HOW TO
DRESS
FOR
SUCCESS

Edith Head
with Joe Hyams

Illustrated by
EDITH HEAD

V&A Publishing

First published by Random House, Inc., New York, 1967
This edition published by V&A Publishing, 2009
Victoria and Albert Museum
South Kensington
London SW7 2RL
www.vandapublishing.com

Hardback edition
ISBN 978 1 851 77554 5

10 9 8 7 6 5
2020 2019 2018

Design by here. www.heredesign.co.uk

Printed in China

V&A Publishing

Supporting the world's leading
museum of art and design,
the Victoria and Albert
Museum, London

CONTENTS

Introduction   **1**

1 How to Dress for Success in Business   **7**

2 How to Dress to Get a Man ...
and Keep Him   **21**

3 How to Dress Your Family for Success   **42**

4 How to Build a Successful Wardrobe   **60**

5 How to Succeed in Looking Younger   **79**

6 How to Analyze Your Figure   **92**

7 How to Use Color Successfully   **107**

8 Success in Fashion Camouflage   **127**

9 The 'Successories' of Your Wardrobe or
Accessories Season the Costume   **133**

10 The 'Secrets of Success' or
Underneath It All   **141**

11 How to Shop for Success   **148**

12 Basic Wardrobe Charts   **154**

13 Nothing Succeeds Like Success   **174**

With thanks to Maybelle Hall
for invaluable editorial assistance

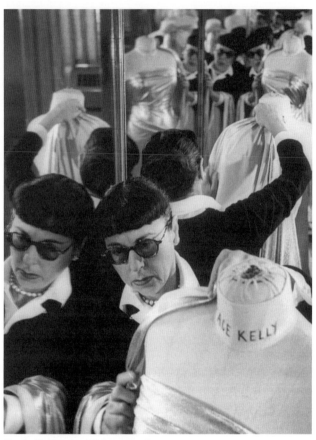

Photo by Allan Grant/Time Life Pictures/Getty Images

Introduction

This book is addressed to women who want Success. And that means to all the women in America who are both old enough to *know* what they want and energetic enough to go after it. We are not talking here solely about success in business. The road to success, feminine-style, is rarely single-tracked. It is a many-laned highway that branches out in various directions. If you are a business woman, of course you want success in your chosen career. But, chances are, your view of the rainbow's end holds more than a crock of gold.

Most women want the warm security of a happy marriage. But feminine success goals are limitless in variety, including social status, the admiration of one's children, the adoration of a husband or boyfriend, prominence in one's community, a reputation for impeccable taste, membership in an exclusive club and many others.

No matter in which direction your strivings for success are pointed, what you wear and how you look can make the difference between moving steadily toward your goal or just rocking back and forth in the same spot. In these days of mass-marketing techniques, you know that when a product lacks eye-appeal it gathers dust on the shelf. So at the very outset, we say 'think of yourself as a product.' In order to achieve success, you have to sell that product, so start right now thinking of how you can improve it.

Your basic virtues, assets, attractions, talents and loving heart may be far and away superior to those of most of your contemporaries. Your family and friends may think you're the greatest thing since Eve—but Eve, remember, had an edge. She was one of a kind, with no competition.

The *you* we're talking about is not alone. She is manufactured by the dozens, the hundreds, the thousands in all sizes and shapes of women, all after success—in many cases, the same success you seek. And in this competitive race, it is frequently the best 'packaging' that makes the difference between those who are left on the shelf and those who are sought after and snapped up fast in the well-stocked supermarket of modern life.

The difference between 'packaging' *you* and a static product like a can of beans is considerable. The beans are going only one place. You are going many places, and the way you look in each special situation, at different times of the day and on varied locations calls for a variety of looks, a number of moods and a diversified wardrobe.

When Hollywood stars dress for specific roles, the clothes they wear are of tremendous importance in projecting the feeling and the personality of each character. It would be pretty hard to take even Lady Macbeth seriously, if she were dressed in a teenie-weenie polka dot bikini—and even the world's greatest sex symbol would hardly rate a whistle gotten up like Whistler's Mother.

Our point is that what you wear at all times must be chosen for appropriateness as well as for flattery. Even a limited wardrobe should include the right things for all possible eventualities in your particular scheme of life. Mix business with pleasure if you wish—but don't wear a cocktail dress to the office, even if you've been out all night.

The way you dress—or package yourself—is the one thing over which you have absolute control. You can't change the size of your feet, the shape of your legs, the color of your eyes or the texture of your hair—but you can change the way you look as easily as an actress does each time she plays a new role.

When you know what you want out of life—the areas of success you desire—then it is easy to dress 'in character' to create the most exciting, pleasing, attractive appearance for your audience. There is no pat recipe for dressing for success, but this book, like a compass, can keep you from getting lost on the pathway to success by steering you away from the Jungle of Bad Taste, the Quicksand of Mediocrity and the Big Bad Wolf of Nothing-to-wear.

In your search for success, of course, clothes cannot take the place of the essential qualities needed for that success. Looking like a super-efficient executive secretary may help you get the job, but it won't help you punctuate the letters. Looking like a perfect homemaker may impress the eligible bachelor you invite to dinner, but it won't disguise the fact that your coffee tastes like hot mud.

Clothes can make you look the part you want to play, but they can't replace the ability to play it. So don't make success impossible by wanting something for which your skills, abilities and talents are hopelessly inadequate. Don't set your heart on a job or a man you can't handle, or can't get. Aim high—but keep your goals achievable.

Above all, face the true facts about yourself. Draw a balance sheet on paper that lists your physical assets and liabilities. If your liabilities seem overwhelming, remember this: in more than twenty years of designing for and dressing the world's most glamorous women for motion pictures, theatre and television, I have yet to meet one who is physically flawless. Most of the beauties you think are perfect have defects just as you do. But they have learned how to accentuate the positive and camouflage the negative.

Women come in a vast variety of recognizable basic types: the cute type, the majestic type, the dainty type, the boyish type, the clinging-vine type, the outdoor-girl type, the sexy type and many others. Decide right now which basic type you are. Ask yourself how big a part your clothes have played in making you that type. Would you rather be a different type? Would you prefer being chic to being cute, looking dramatic to looking majestic, appearing more feminine, less mousey, more striking? What you wear, more than any other factor, can improve the type you are or *change your type* completely.

It is of first importance that the look you long for be compatible with your success goal. Does it fit into the picture of you moving rapidly toward the role you eventually want to play?

These are questions only *you* can answer. But once answered, this book can help you emphasize your assets, minimize your liabilities and create the image you desire, to achieve your heart's desire.

Throughout my career I have used clothes to turn drudges into princesses, plain Janes into glamor girls, frumps into fashion plates. As one of my star friends insists, 'If Cinderella had Edith Head, she'd never have needed a Fairy Godmother.'

So there you are. If you know what you want from life, I know how to help you get it.

Let's put our heads together and move forward!

1

How to Dress for
SUCCESS IN BUSINESS

1. How to Dress for Success in Business

Success in business means different things to different women. To some women and girls, their business lives are merely intervals between the time they leave school and the time they get married. To them a successful business career is a short one, leading not to the front office with a golden name on the door, but straight to the altar with a golden ring on the finger. If you are in this group, we devote the entire next chapter to you. But in the meantime we suggest you make the most of your success story at the office by reading this chapter too. Who knows, you might marry the boss!

GETTING THE JOB

Before you even select the first article of clothing involved, you have to know what kind of job you want. There are vast differences in the kinds of dressing desired (and required) by different kinds of business firms. In larger organizations where dependability, solidity and integrity overshadow glamor (for instance, banks, insurance companies, law offices or blue-chip industrial corporations) a far more conservative type of dressing is prevalent than in business offices of a more imaginative and creative bent (such as advertising, publishing, merchandising or the entertainment field).

To get the job you want in the field you feel best equipped for, spend some time finding out about it. Learn all you can about it by reading, asking questions, following the business notes in the daily newspaper, and by getting your hands on some of the trade papers and magazines read by people in that field.

A few issues of *The Wall Street Journal*, for instance, will give you a veneer of knowledge about the financial community—as will such publications as *Advertising Age*, *Petroleum News*, *The Law Journal*, and *Women's Wear Daily* about the respective fields for which they are published. If the city you live in doesn't have such publications on the newsstands, go to the library to bone up on them.

The more you know about the type of business you want to become part of, the more intelligently you will be able to handle the interview you eventually get. If you have narrowed down your job goal to a specific company, try to get your hands on their last Annual Report (from a bank or stockbroker) and study it. It will fill you in on pertinent facts about the company's products or services, growth pattern, position in the industry, policies, and so on.

All this information, plus how you are dressed for your interview, will stand you in very good stead and help your chances for getting the job you want.

THE ACCEPTANCE LOOK

What you wear for that interview will also depend to some extent on the caliber of job you're after. It is obvious that if you are being interviewed for a secretarial position that pays from $65 to $100 a week, wearing a $5,000 mink coat or lavish jewelry will not be good judgment even if your father is a millionaire. We talked to numerous personnel directors in preparing this book, and their consensus of opinion is that in hiring young women for secretarial or other clerical work, they want people that fit in with the general character of the organization and with the other personnel. Obviously, a girl with a millionairess's wardrobe could only incur envy and animosity among a group of girls less richly endowed.

Personnel directors try to avoid inter-office jealousies created by inequities of this kind, and prefer new employees that fit the image already in existence. Extremism in make-up, hairdos, length of skirts or brilliance of color are likely to be frowned on. The interviewer will think, 'This one has just cooked too long—she's overdone in every way.' Simplicity and good taste are the rules in applying for any job, plus the immaculate grooming that speaks louder than words about how neat and careful a girl will be in her work.

The basic elements of any business woman's wardrobe should rely on this trio: simple casual suits, tailored dresses and good separates (shirts, blouses, sweaters and other tops). For specific guidance, you'll find detailed lists in Chapter 12.

Before you are interviewed for the job you want, try on the complete outfit you intend to wear. Look at yourself in the mirror from every angle, including *sitting down* which is the way you will look most of the time to the person who will make the decision. Ask yourself these questions: (a) Do I look well groomed? (b) Do I look neat? (c) Do I feel comfortable and at ease? (d) Does my skirt ride up too much? (e) Have I worn too much (or too little) make-up or jewelry? (f) Does this outfit really fit the image of the position I hope to fill?

We have known of instances where extremely capable women failed to get a job because they looked *too* elegantly put together. One personnel director confided to us in a specific case, 'I didn't hire her simply because I felt anyone that looked that attractive would have a date every night in the week and would never be free to stay until 5:15 in an emergency.'

This doesn't mean that dressing to get a job should be an effort to make yourself *less* attractive. It means you should look your *best*—but your *business* best rather than your beau-catching best.

aim for success!

Vast changes have taken place in the last twenty years in 'types' of dressing. Remember when the very word 'schoolteacher' conjured up a vision of a hard-bitten, flat-chested, flat-heeled, bespectacled female with no more sex appeal than a dishpan? Gone are those days. Schoolteachers today look as pretty and fashionable as other business women, but they don't come into the classroom done up like Sex Goddesses.

In the movie industry the same changes have taken place. Costuming relies much more on reality than on fantasy. Having dressed thousands of actors and actresses for every conceivable type of role, I can tell you that we too have made mistakes in judgment. Once upon a time glamor was the costume requirement of every movie star in every part, whether or not the role called for it. In the Thirties, Carole Lombard was costumed for the role of a little secretary practically dripping with pearls and sables. Today people would laugh out loud at such a characterization. Now, with far more sophisticated audiences, a great deal of research is done to make sure that every actor or actress is dressed the way he or she would be dressed for the actual situation.

To make a movie credible to its audience, stars must be dressed properly and authentically for the activities in which they are involved. Doris Day as a schoolteacher was dressed differently from Shirley MacLaine as a magazine writer. Elizabeth Taylor as a clerk in a bookstore was wardrobed in a different manner from Jane Wyman as a department store executive. Eva Gabor as a fashion stylist had an entirely different look from Julie Andrews as a scientist or Anne Bancroft as a secretary.

When we are involved in a scene where a girl works at Lockheed, we don't guess about what she should wear. We go to Lockheed and find out. If she is portraying the part of a banker's secretary, we send scouts to banks to see what the going garb is in such inner sanctums.

In *Love for a Proper Stranger* we had to dress Natalie Wood as a salesgirl in the pet department at Macy's. We went straight to Macy's and shopped for a hamster. We saw that the girls who handled animals all wore a certain kind of smock. We got a sample of it and copied it exactly.

Today people expect this kind of authenticity in theatrical costuming—and they expect the same kind of 'fitness for the occasion' in everything you wear too.

In Hollywood we call this aspect of costuming the 'acceptance look'—a good term to have in your own wardrobe vocabulary.

Naturally if the business you want to break into is a field where fashion flair, color co-ordination and ideas are essential, you should make a point of dressing to play up these talents, in keeping with the job. For example, if you were applying for a position as assistant buyer in the sportswear department of a large department store, it would just be silly to go in for the interview in anything but a handsome sportswear outfit, such as a good knitted dress or tweed separates.

In the picture *Houseboat* I was called upon to dress that exciting Sophia Loren as, of all things, a mousey little housekeeper. Believe me, this took more doing than turning Olive Oyl into a sex symbol. It's harder to make a sow's ear out of a silk purse than vice versa. Sophia said, 'Please, Edith, make me look as though I really am this poor, overworked woman. I want to be believed in completely.' A few weeks later, when she saw the rushes of the scene, she said, 'Edith, that's marvelous; if that woman was sent to me for a job as a housekeeper—I'd hire her!'

We ask you to project some of these experiences into your own scheme of things in job-getting. Analyze the kind of business you're attempting to break into—find out the 'acceptance look' for that industry or company, and package yourself to it.

Again you have to have a specific goal in mind. What does getting ahead mean—merely getting a $5 raise every six months? Or does it mean moving gradually or quickly up the ladder to genuine career status—private secretary to the president—private office of your own—or whatever is your goal?

It is obvious that a too-impatient attitude and a too-driving nature in the race for success can propel you backwards through the door you came in. So don't let everyone know you think you're cut out for better things. Let *them* find it out. There's no need to hide your light under a bushel of modesty either. The important thing in your progress toward the better job you want is to get there on the path that avoids stepping on other people's toes. Remember those aching toes can retaliate by tripping you up on the way to success. So watch them.

Above all, do your present job perfectly, to the utmost of your capacity. Many a ball game has been lost because of an overeager second baseman who is so anxious to throw the ball that he fails to catch it first. If you learn how to do the job at hand with excellence and thoroughness, you will not only have a better chance of moving ahead to a better job, but you will be equipping yourself for a better future in every area—including marriage.

If you have what it takes—in talent, skill and personality—and you know where you want to go in a specific area, our advice is start working on it *now*. Take some night courses in subjects that will ready you for that important upward step. What subjects will help you most in that coveted spot: Accounting? Merchandising? Public speaking? A foreign language? Marketing? Salesmanship?

If courses on the subjects you need are not available in your city, *read* all about them. Haunt the library for books that will help you to be a self-made woman. And at the same time, start to dress up to the part.

This new on-the-way-up situation, unlike the initial one of *getting* the job, allows you much more leeway in the way you dress. First of all, once you have established your worth to the company and want to be considered for a position with greater status, you can step a little bit out of the picture frame that holds the 'acceptance look' into what might be called the 'executive look.'

No doubt you will have noticed that the female executives in your chosen field make a point of dressing a little differently from the run-of-the-mill office girls. Where the girls in the stenographic pool come into the office in sweaters and skirts, the executive in charge wears a completely co-ordinated costume. Where the receptionist may go to lunch with a scarf over her head and no gloves, the executive-to-be wears a smart hat and gloves, if only to set herself apart from the crowd.

She eschews 'faddy' here-today-gone-tomorrow styles for things that reflect quality and taste. She resists the desire to have a lot of changes in her wardrobe in order to concentrate on fewer, more elegantly fashioned costumes that do more for her, and which are not in the lookalike wardrobes of the other girls. She invests in clothes which are not strikingly different, but which are intrinsically finer.

The feminine executive is no longer a phenomenon in our society. More and more businesses are recognizing the equal-to-men talents of women in top-echelon jobs, and while the opportunity to reach such high positions is open to only the exceptional individual, looking the part is of even more importance at this level. The reasons are obvious. In an executive capacity, a woman in business meets more people from the outside. She is called upon, perhaps, to entertain customers, handle difficult situations, exercise authority. She lunches with and is socially accepted by other executives, both male and female. She can no longer afford to look like one of the girls in the office.

At the same time she cannot afford to overlook the organization she is part of, any more than a male executive can. Nobody cares much, for instance, if the stockboy comes to work on a hot day in a short-sleeved sports shirt with no jacket, but woe be unto the rising young assistant vice-president who sits in his air-conditioned office in sneakers and no necktie.

By the same token, the appearance you make on your rise to success must be in keeping with both where you are and where you want to go. This imposes some hardships on you, perhaps, in comparison to the carefree little file clerk whom nobody sees. She can be stockingless, girdleless, gloveless, hatless and shiftless with far less danger than you can. You have something to live up to: your future success in the exciting job you want most.

When you reach the top rung it's a different story. The eccentricities of the genius who is top man (or woman) on the totem pole of tycoonery are not only condoned but admired. What you wear when you sit in the president's chair is entirely up to you. At that point you can give this book to your assistant and make notes on what you'll wear as chairman of the board.

On the way up, however, distinction without flamboyance should be your credo. And don't be trapped by your own desire to follow the crowd by wearing the last scream of fashion. Subdue that urge to buy what merchants call a 'hot number.' This is the dress or suit that is copied in every price level and winds up in the closet of every third girl in the office.

When every other girl in the office has decided to wear her hair up or teased or straight to the shoulders—that's the time for you to achieve a new and distinctive look. When the current make-up theme is 'doe eyes' or 'two pairs of lashes' or 'pale lips' or 'hollow cheeks,' resist—desist— and be *yourself*. Wear the make-up that does the most for *you* while everyone else in the office projects a single monotonous pattern.

There is always a subtle difference between those who lead and those who are led. If your energies and executive abilities place you at the front of the parade, don't wear a private's uniform.

Now for a few suggestions to both the job-hunters and the career-minded. A good cookbook may be able to give a cut-and-dried recipe for salad dressing, but there is no set of measured ingredients for success dressing. In many cases you have to experiment. Try it, taste it, add a little, take away a little and change it until it's right.

However, there is one rule that must never be overlooked. It is simply, 'Get Organized.' First, organize your *purchases*. Don't be carried away by that cute little orange dress when you have no suitable shoes, bag, gloves or hat to go with it, unless you can afford a complete set of accessories for every outfit. Work out your color schemes carefully *before* you buy so that accessories can be interchanged and every costume you wear presents a complete picture from head to toe.

Second, organize *yourself* for each day's activities. It takes only a few minutes every night, but often makes the difference between giving an impression of thrown-together carelessness or a look of perfection. A mad scramble in the morning, wildly pulling things out and dressing like a house on fire will get you nothing but high blood pressure. And speaking of a house on fire, who ever heard of a fireman not laying out his clothes before he goes to bed? He just jumps into them and slides down the pole. You might not be able to match him in speed, but you can arrive at the office every morning calm, cool, collected and *on time*. A good way, by the way, to keep from *being* fired.

How do you do it? First, review what your next day's activities are going to be. Business before pleasure of course, but consider also your lunch date, cocktail date and dinner date, if any. Pick the basic dress or suit or costume that will work for all three. Lay out the shoes, handbag, hosiery, jewelry, gloves—everything you need for the office.

If there's any doubt about how the costume fits you or the length of the skirt, try it on to make sure. It's better to switch the night before than to start all over in the morning.

If you have after-hours activities on that day, select something right for the office that can be dressed-up for your date. It's amazing what a softer blouse and pretty jewelry can do for a simple suit. Carry with you dressier gloves and a glamorous cocktail hat, and you have it made. The extras will all fit neatly into your hatbox or tote bag, so you can switch on the glamor after five.

SUCCESS FORMULA FOR HOW TO DRESS
TO GET AND GET AHEAD ON A JOB

1. Decide what kind of job you really want and prepare yourself for it.

2. Decide if you are qualified for it. If not, look for one you can handle.

3. Find out the 'image' of the job—how women in that field or firm look and dress. Ask someone who works there. If you don't know anyone, go at noontime or at 5 P.M. and watch the women who work there leaving. Find out the general 'look' of the employees.

4. Dress carefully for your appointment in what you have found is the generally accepted look.

5. Above all, be well groomed and look like a girl or woman who would be a credit to the firm. Then do a good job!

2

How to Dress to
GET A MAN...
and Keep Him

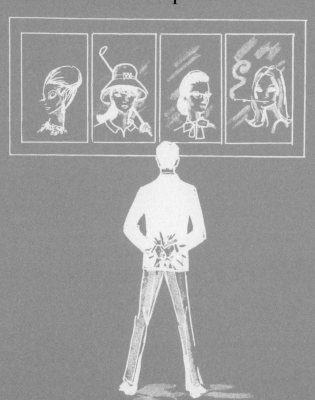

2. How to Dress to Get a Man … and Keep Him

The contents of this chapter may be a shock to the woman who feels that the less she wears in pursuit of a man the better. To her we can only say that while the boys ogle and applaud the charms of Venus Unadorned in art galleries, night clubs and between the covers of some magazines, it's the covered girls rather than the Cover Girls they invariably marry. Man is a possessive animal by nature and cares little about sharing his wealth of wifely treasure with the wolf-pack. And corny as it may seem in our free-wheeling society where topless bathing suits, bottom-revealing pants and above-the-knee skirts abound, most men shudder at the thought of their wives as striptease artists—beyond the master's bedroom, that is.

When you place yourself on the launching pad, pointed toward the great adventure of matrimony, please be realistic and pick a goal you can reach. Falling in love with a man so famous, so rich or so handsome that you're unlikely ever to meet him is simply propelling yourself toward heartbreak. Even if you did manage to get into orbit with such a paragon, consider the difficulties of keeping up with him as you fight off the competition. Look all around you for a man to marry rather than star-gazing. Count the available men you see every day—at the office, at church, at the railroad station, at the skating rink, the country club or the beach. *One of them may be just for you.* Ask yourself if you measure up to the challenge of attracting him with what you wear *every* day.

In spite of the oft-repeated phrase mouthed by everyone's Aunt Tillie that 'all men are alike,' we urge you to start on your husband quest by discarding this notion instantly. The only way all eligible men are alike (regardless of size, shape, personality or financial standing) is in their desire to stay in the lead and to avoid the altar while being chased by some woman, or more likely, by several. Men, dear reader, are very much in demand. Statistics prove that (1) women outlive them by at least three years, leaving a growing residue of eager widows to add to the already sizable pool of mate-hungry women, and (2) there are 3,617,545 more unattached women than men in the United States (single, separated, divorced and widowed). (In Australia, the picture is in reverse, in case you want to go there.)

THAT FIRST MEETING

Before advising you on how to dress to get a husband we must, of course, assume that you already know an eligible man—a man you would like to marry.

If you don't know the man, or haven't met him, do what a hunter does. Go where the game is! We've heard many sad tales of unattached girls taking costly cruises to romantic places only to find themselves in the same boat with six hundred other miserable females, all vying for the overworked attentions of the three bachelors on board. One such bachelor confided to me that his theme song in this mêlée was 'Good Night, A Thousand Good Nights.'

We've also shed tears over the laments of girls who spent an entire year's savings at plushy resorts where the huntresses outnumbered the quarry ten to one. Our advice to these women is very practical. If you just can't meet any men in your own town or city, pack up your vacation wardrobe and go to a convention hotel. Pick the convention where you'd be likely to meet the kind of man you think you'd like. Bankers, lawyers, doctors, dentists, plumbers, printers, publishers and advertising men all attend conventions by the hundreds.

If this doesn't appeal to you, you might try spending your vacation traveling back and forth on a train or plane that plies between two points well-traversed by businessmen. For example, you could take any non-stop flight between New York, Chicago, Los Angeles or San Francisco. By railroad you could try the Merchants' from New York to Boston. But before you take such drastic measures, consider the possibilities near at hand. Do you live near a university? Take some night courses. Do you play cards? Join a card club or take a Bridge Cruise. Do you like to dance? Take a series of dance lessons at one of the major dance studios. Do you like sports? Indulge your interest by participating *actively*. Skating, skiing, tennis, golf, archery or any other sport can place you 'where the game is' in more ways than one.

It goes without saying that what you wear in any of these pursuits is of vital importance in sparking the meeting. If you're traveling, your costume must be impeccable, your luggage interesting and your reading matter carefully chosen to invite conversation.

Under no circumstances allow your seat companion to see you reading this chapter!

If you're going out for your favorite sport, be sure your costume measures up to your performance on the court, the rink, the links or the slope.

'But,' you may say, 'why would any man want to meet *me*? I'm far from beautiful, and just not the type they turn around to look at.' Our answer is simply that very few women are sensationally beautiful. If you can make yourself *interesting* to look at and *interesting to be with* your attraction for the opposite sex will be more than satisfactory.

Frequently at parties and premières attended by Hollywood stars, visitors are shocked when they see the wives of our handsomest film stars. These men, who work constantly with women who are the epitome of glamor, very often marry girls who are quite ordinary to look at. The unknowing are inclined to comment, 'How on earth did *she* ever get *him*?'

I can tell you, because I know. She *interested* him more than other women.

Have you ever analyzed what makes the most interesting people you know interesting? Chances are it is the fact that they are *interested* in *you*. The same principle works with men. The most fascinating woman in the world, to any man, is the woman who is sincerely, truly interested in *him*.

It's obvious that you can't really show how interested you are in a man unless you know something about him. This is the second step, once you've met him.

GETTING TO KNOW HIM

You've spotted your game now, Diana, and you want to bring him back alive—with an engagement ring in his paw. What's the bait that will make him follow you to the ends of the earth or propel you down the aisle to the strains of Lohengrin? Getting to know him, getting to know all about him, as one of the lovely songs from *The King and I* so aptly put it. Draw him out; discover his interests, idiosyncrasies, likes and dislikes. If possible, try to find out who his favorite actresses are in motion pictures, television and the theater. This might be your clue to the types he likes. Ask him why he likes these stars. Is it the way they look, the way they talk, the parts they play? You'll learn a lot about that man simply by listening. Don't forget, however, that a much too aggressive attitude and too many pointed questions might scare him away. So by all means be subtle. Be *interested*, not inquisitive.

So much for the psychology of the first meeting. Now let's consider the first date—inevitable outcome of the successful meeting. Here's where what you wear comes into play even more importantly.

If he tells you exactly where he's taking you, the solution to the question of what to wear is quite simple. When you know he has box seats for a much-heralded concert, opera or ballet, you know you'll be safe in your prettiest short evening dress, white kid gloves and most elegant jewelry.

But suppose he merely invites you to have dinner with him on Saturday night. You can't ask him, 'Where?' or 'How much money do you plan to spend?' You probably don't even know how much money he has. This is the time where good judgment must take over. If you wear your prettiest short evening dress when he planned to take you to a small inexpensive restaurant that caters to the family trade, one of two things will happen: (1) you'll be miserably uncomfortable all through dinner and fail to be any fun as a companion, or (2) he'll change his original plans and feel forced to take you someplace more in keeping with your costume, in which case he'll think your tastes are too rich for his bank account. Either way this first date is likely to be the last.

However, if you consider all the possibilities before you dress for that first date, you can be perfectly dressed for almost any eventuality. This is called playing it safe. Select a simple dress from your wardrobe that can be dressed up or down. Adorn it with attractive, but not lavish, jewelry. If, when he comes to pick you up, he mentions going somewhere where there's music and dancing, you can change your jewelry—put on a little evening hat or headdress and add your most party-festive coat or fur. If he says you're just going to the movies, leave well enough alone and wear your daytime coat, plus a colorful and interesting scarf.

But suppose he's meeting you right at the office and you have no clue where you'll be going from there. Should you wear that pretty semi-dressy dark dress to the office and follow the same course? No, indeed. In such an eventuality, there's nothing that can top a soft suit with high-buttoned jacket in a flattering, feminine color like soft blue, beige, gray or rose. With the jacket on, you are well dressed for business, but underneath your jacket is glamor you can switch on as needed. It is a pretty, dressy shell overblouse—sleeveless if you have attractive arms, with cap sleeves if you don't. Have a jewelled pin or necklace and earrings tucked in your handbag. If your evening turns out to be a big one (a party, a plush candle-lit restaurant or a night club) off goes the jacket and on go the jewels. If nothing more exciting develops than a hamburger with french fries—don't open a single button of that jacket, and keep the jewels concealed!

Either way, you have it made—and you're on the way to a second date for sure.

But let's face it, a soft dark dress and a soft pastel suit don't make a wardrobe. These are merely the staples that belong in every woman's closet. The building of the right wardrobe for every occasion on your big game hunt for a husband depends on the *man*. Men fall readily into five categories or types. If you have been doing your homework in finding out all about him, you can easily decide which group your man fits into and then dress accordingly. Instead of shopping madly for a lot of new clothes selected without plan, buy with *him* in mind. So let's get down to cases and talk about *him*. (Remember—he *adores* it when you do.)

Is he the *Outdoor Type* or *Sportsman*?

Without much effort you will be able to find out if he's this type at your first meeting. The sportsman talks about his favorite sport with little or no encouragement. But don't think just because he's hipped on Arnold Palmer or the Yankees that you know all about him. There are subtle and very important differences between sports lovers that can easily lead a gal astray in her desire to please him.

For instance, there's the active sportsman and the spectator sportsman.

First let's take the active sportsman, as opposed to the man who simply follows sporting events. Let's say your man is mad about tennis. His conversation is so love-oriented you might think all you need to do is buy a racket and a pair of sneakers to make him think you're Margaret Smith. However, if you happen to have two left feet on a tennis court and your serve bounces around like Silly Putty, for heaven's sake *don't* play tennis with him! Be a marvelous spectator instead, and dress the part. Buy yourself some charming spectator costumes—crisp, fresh and neat—and learn all you can about tennis and tennis personalities. It's better to talk a good game than play a poor one.

If your man happens to love duck hunting, don't rush out to equip yourself with gun, poncho and rubber boots until you know what kind of *women* he likes. Some of the most rugged sportsmen we know just can't stand competitive women.

If he's this type, women are taboo on fishing trips, anathema on the golf course and excess baggage on a bear hunt. He's one of the strong men who likes his women weak. He wants to pursue his game with the boys and come home to a little woman who is waiting, wide-eyed, to hear (by the hour) the details of how he caught that swordfish, made that hole-in-one or stalked that grizzly. Such men want their women *feminine*, and the only pants they want to see you in are sexy hostess pajamas.

There are, of course, active sportsmen who want their women to excel in their chosen sport and to be their constant playmates. If your man is this type, you'd better make a decision. Say skiing is his first love, and you suffer from acrophobia. You either have to conquer your fear of heights or spend every weekend alone.

If he wants to play twenty-seven holes of golf every Saturday and you have weak arches, make up your mind. Either you suffer around that course with a smile on your face or you take the chance of losing that man. (They say walking is therapeutic for tortured tootsies, so you might wind up with good feet *plus* a good husband.)

If you are interested enough in both the man and the game, you're really on the way to making your goal. But it also takes the right wardrobe. When a man takes a sport seriously, he knows that the right clothes are important not only as status symbols, but as part of the equipment for performing like a pro. This type of man is quick to spot the wrong kind of golf shoes, out-of-date ski pants, cheap riding boots or an ill-fitting skating dress. He *knows* the score on active sports clothes and expects you to know it too. If you're in doubt about what to wear with him, go to a good store that specializes in active sports fashions and find out. If there's no such store near you, write to Abercrombie & Fitch in New York. You'll get excellent advice and guidance and a wardrobe worthy of a pro. And once you know which sports are his favorites, subscribe to magazines that will keep you abreast of what's happening and who makes the news in these areas.

On the other side of the sportsman's coin, let's picture all the men who follow a particular sport without actively participating. They're the baseball fans, the hockey hounds, the football maniacs, the polo fiends, the boxing buffs, the bowling, basketball and racetrack followers. They know the name of every player on every team, and woe be to the woman (or man) who doesn't share their enthusiasm for their chosen sport. To interest this type of sportsman, the sporting pages of the daily newspapers are required reading for you. If you get on the wire with this type, be prepared to spend your evenings and weekends watching his favorite sport either on television or at the scene. If he only watches on television, just look pretty and keep quiet. But if he has to *see* every game in person you can be sure he has the right wardrobe for spectating (slacks, tweed jackets, handsome sports shirts and sweaters), so don't show up at the stadium dressed for frugging. Concentrate on good casual sports separates, comfortable shoes, good leather handbags and colorful scarfs, and the two of you will look like a pair that really came packaged together.

And above all, if he's a football fan—dress warmly! There's nothing more revolting to the rugged gridiron enthusiast than a shivering, complaining female whose only comment about the game is, 'I'm freezing!' Dress in layers—you can always remove sweaters, socks or boots if the temperature rises, but don't expect him to bundle you into his arms to warm you up when he's all wrapped up in that forward pass.

At *any* sporting event, whether it's racing, football, hockey, tennis, polo or ping-pong, if you ask him, 'What's happening?' when the crowd cheers, your romance is over. If you don't know what's happening, keep quiet—unless he's cheering. In that case, cheer too.

Now let's consider another type—The *Sophisticated Man-about-town*. A far cry from the sportsman—although he's a sport in other areas—is the man who has many interests. He is aware of everything that's in, from the latest discotheque dances to the hit musical shows. He has read this month's best-seller and knows the head waiter in all the best restaurants. He prides himself on his good taste, and he's a perfectionist. Invariably he is articulate and entertaining as a conversationalist. This makes it essential for you to be a good listener. But don't think you can get away with dumb, adoring silence forever. He expects an intelligent comment once in a while. And he is attracted, like all men, to women who are interested in the things that interest him.

Because his interests are manifold, there's more homework for you to do with this type of man than most others. Reading one or more of the weekly news magazines each week will keep you up to date on many things that interest him: books, personalities, shows, fashions, politics. If you aren't an avid reader of novels, at least read the book reviews, so when he asks what you think of Auchincloss and Bellow, you don't say, 'You mean the lawyers?'

If you haven't read a book or seen a play he starts discussing, for heaven's sake *don't say you have*. When he starts questioning you about which character you sympathized with and whether you agreed with the viewpoint expressed at the end, your answers are likely to reveal you as a phoney. Be honest; tell him you haven't read it, but would like him to tell you about it. He'll be not only flattered, but delighted to give you his condensed version.

Like the sportsman, this type of man splits, like an amoeba, into two distinct subtypes: (A) The Super-sophisticate and (B) The Hail-fellow-well-met.

Subtype A inclines toward subdued elegance in everything and is something of a snob about anything too overdone or too noisy, too jazzy or too *anything*. In dressing to please him, ask yourself these three questions: Is it chic? Is it ladylike? Does it suggest quiet elegance?

If he takes you out dancing (which he most certainly will) he doesn't mind if people turn around to stare at you if you look simply smashing—but he'll steer you to the darkest corner if you look too bizarre.

He likes dark or subtle colors, small patterns, luxurious fabrics and perfectly put-together costumes. He prefers the look of one magnificent piece of fashion jewelry on an utterly simple dress to a dazzling array of bracelets that make you sound like a big brass band. He notices that you're wearing leather, rather than fabric gloves, and appreciates the fact that you carry a pretty handkerchief instead of a package of tissues. He is a proud man and wants to be proud of his women.

Wearing the right thing at the right time is of greater importance to him than to most other men, because he knows more about the right thing. A less knowledgeable man might not know the difference between a cocktail dress and a dinner gown, but this man does. And he will be careful to tell you whether your date is for cocktails or an informal dinner. If he tells you, 'It's a black-tie affair,' don't ask him if it's a funeral.

Even though he is a man-about-town, sooner or later he will expect you to entertain *him*. At this point, remember he has been entertained by some of the best huntresses in town because, after all, he *is* that most desirable of all creatures—an *extra* man. How you handle this first invitation to your home can spell triumph or catastrophe for your romance.

The people you invite, the hors d'oeuvres you serve, the glasses you use, the menu you plan will all be carefully noted by this man who is measuring your qualifications (you hope) as the possible chatelaine of his future chateau. He may adore the way you dance, be delighted with your French accent, and be simply sent by the way you flutter your eyelashes, but if you turn out to be a dud in the drawing room, his disenchantment will be immediate and irrevocable.

So for this first invitation to meet your friends and sample your cooking, don't bite off more than you can chew. Make it a small intimate group of people, six to eight at most, who are interested in the same things he is (that includes nearly everything). A buffet menu will make things easier for you unless you have a staff of servants or good part-time help. Choose the records in advance (soft background piano music) and don't serve champagne if you have only sherry glasses.

What should you wear? Something he has never seen before, of course. This is his special introduction to the at-home you—the 'you' he'll come home to every night (you hope) with a heart full of joy.

A full-length hostess gown in a color that blends with your living room is the perfect answer, but make sure it is one you can move in gracefully without spilling the drinks, tripping over the skirt or knocking over the candles. When you choose it, bear in mind how busy you will be as a hostess, so don't select something with long tight sleeves and a high turtle neck that will make you look and feel like a steamed clam after the first cocktail. Play it cool. And no matter how glamorous they look in the ads, avoid long dangling necklaces that wind up in the salad bowl when you're serving. Above all, for every three cocktails you serve your guests, make a weak one on the rocks for yourself. There's nothing that will turn a potential bride into a passing fancy quicker than her passing out at her own party.

Now for subtype B in our man-about-town category, *The Hail-fellow-well-met*. He's sometimes known as 'Good Time Charlie.' He is a little less meticulous than the Super-sophisticate about the right thing and the right place. He's out for fun and laughs. He dances with more abandon, drinks a little more, laughs a little louder and works a lot faster than our friend, Type A. He's the complete extrovert who will keep the conversational ball bouncing all evening whether you say anything or not. Just laugh at his jokes and he'll think you're wonderful. His taste in girls is more flamboyant in every way. If this is the man you're after, consider becoming a blonde or a redhead. Pile on the bracelets—he likes noise. Rather than seeking out the most elegant clothes to please him, find things that have youthful verve, like short flippy skirts, bright zingy colors and cute crazy hats. He's the eternal 'boy' who never wants to grow old. When he takes you out on the town you're likely to hop from a bohemian beer joint to a hot jazz festival to a hootenanny to a bowling alley.

'Anything for kicks' is his motto, so don't dress for him as though you belong under glass. Let him know you're as fun-loving as he is, and wear clothes that look and feel *young*.

'Is he the marrying kind?' you may ask. (Ask yourself, of course, don't ask *him*.) Well, girl, there is really no such thing! He doesn't want to get married any more than the next fellow, or the fellow next to him. But if he has a wonderful time every time he's with you, he'll want to be with you *all* the time. Particularly if you laugh at his jokes the *second* time he tells them.

As different from Good Time Charlie as a martini is from a malted milk is Type Number Three—*The Shy Conservative Man*. You will recognize him by his quiet, unassuming manner, his soft-spoken voice, his solid color neckties, definite opinions and the relaxing fact that he doesn't proposition you on your first date. With this man, anything overt or obvious in your actions, conversation or wearing apparel will send him scurrying back to the serenity of his lonely pad and all the blessings of bachelorhood.

Conservatism in your wardrobe will stand you in good stead with this man. Shy away from plunging necklines, black lace textured hosiery, above-the-knee skirts, figure-revealing silhouettes and wild hairdos. To him what fashion editors call 'mod' is merely mad. He wants to see you looking like a lady, perhaps on the plain side. Loud plaids and bold checks shock him as much as loud laughter and risqué jokes. He likes clothes that are inconspicuous, introverted in color, design and pattern. Stick to the classics and you'll make him happy.

If your personality is too outgoing for such a man and dressing to please him would inhibit your desire for expression, look around for Type Number Four—*The Far-Out Intellectual*. What would be the shy man's chloroform is this man's meat. He's a long-hair and doesn't mind if you wear yours down your back. Avant-garde ideas and art nouveau are a delight to his eye—so if he's in your picture, let yourself go on exciting modern prints, exotic color combinations, unusual handmade jewelry and anything that might be called 'artistic' or offbeat. Conservatism in any form is just plain corn to him, so don't be square enough to wear conventional-looking costumes for his sake. He goes for Pop art, Op art, modern ballets—and girls who make the scene with him can look as kookie as they wish.

Type Number Five (everybody's dreamboat) is *The Successful Executive*. He's the man who has it made. If you're lucky enough to have latched onto or even sighted one of this dwindling and rare species, work fast. You can be sure plenty of other women have a bead on him too. Whatever his business interests, he didn't get where he is just goofing off or waiting for things to happen. He is a very definite man. He knows what he likes and dislikes and he makes fast decisions. He is impeccably neat and extremely well organized and simply can't abide sloppy, lazy, disorderly females. He will expect you to be immaculate always. When you have a date with him, don't dawdle around looking for your keys, your handkerchief, your gloves or your glasses while he waits for you. Don't giggle. Sit up straight. And *be on time!*

As to your wardrobe in attracting such a man, it should express luxury without ostentation. He respects quality in investments and in women's clothing. Sacrifice variety in shopping to please him, and settle for intrinsic value in a few blue-chip costumes that will take you proudly wherever he wants to go. One beautifully tailored suit with several blouses to vary its look will cover a lot of ground. This man would rather own one Mercedes Benz and keep it for six years than buy a new car every year. He feels the same way about clothes. He will admire your good taste and good sense for buying one beautiful outfit rather than four short-lived inexpensive ones. He will expect you to be dressed perfectly for dinner in town, or for cocktails at the country club, with very little advance notice. When he phones you at 11 A.M. to meet him for lunch, you'd better have the right thing in your closet or on your back. And when he waltzes you around the dance floor crooning '*Your* time is *my* time' into your pearly ear—he means every word!

Of course, if you're so ravishingly beautiful and sexy that this man (and every other) is panting with passion every time he looks at you, you can break *all* the rules— break dates, arrive late, forget appointments— and he'll forgive you. But are you that irresistible? And, if you are, why are you reading this book anyway?

There are, of course, other types of men you have to take into consideration but they are less likely to be influenced by what you wear. Among these are (A) *The Hungry Man* whose main interest is food. All you need to please him is a well-filled larder and a stove. Wear any old apron, and if your cooking is reasonably good, he'll propose; and (B) *The Drinking Man* whose four martinis before lunch and six before dinner make it nearly impossible for him to see what you're wearing anyway. With him just concentrate on the ice cubes.

Well, you've met your man and you've landed him. Next step: The honeymoon.

HOW TO HOLD ON TO THAT HUSBAND

The habits of some new brides on that most idyllic of all vacations were a great shock to me on a recent trip to Bermuda. The month was June, and the hotels and beaches were filled with honeymooners. With very few exceptions, all the brides made their daytime appearances with their hair up in rollers. The picture they made at the breakfast table, riding bicycles, picnicking on the beach and sightseeing gave the impression that we'd just been invaded by Mars. An assortment of weird, unattractive, bubble-headed, ugly creatures was all over the place —and their poor, too-soon-suffering spouses looked as frightened as the conquered males they were. By dinnertime, however, these same girls emerged from their cocoons as full-blown butterflies, with hair carefully coiffed and make-up adroitly applied, to make the dancetime rounds of the hotels on the arms of their beloveds. This was the only time we saw the young husbands looking really unworried.

We wondered about the effects of this strange new phenomenon of freakishness on the honeymoon, and whether it has anything to do with the current divorce rate of three out of five marriages. Did those few candlelit hours of nighttime glamor make up (in the young men's eyes) for the long sunlit days with nothing to look at but a wife with a head full of scrap metal?

Ask any man and he'll tell you he hates to see a woman with her hair in curlers. He might not talk much about it, but he also instinctively dislikes old, tired-looking bedroom slippers beside the bed, rumpled dressing gowns thrown over chairs and the tacky look of a short robe over a long nightgown at the breakfast table. It doesn't matter which type of man he is (conservative, sportsman, executive, whoever), he wants to think of his wife as fresh, dainty and desirable at all times. To deny him this privilege is as destructive to his ego as telling him you should have married Henry Klotz who now drives a Cadillac.

Whether you are a bride of a few weeks or the mother of a grown family, the way you look to your husband every day should be a matter of personal pride. With today's easy-to-care-for, drip-dry fashions there is no need to wear a nightgown, a housecoat or a daytime dress until it looks as though it, and you, have been through the wringer. No matter how much housework you do yourself, you can look neat, clean and fresh in the presence of your spouse.

I'm sure you've heard friends complain about their husbands, saying, 'When I go to a lot of trouble to get all dressed up in something new, he doesn't even notice it.' Well, the chances are he so rarely sees her looking 'all dressed up,' that he has long since developed a mental block about seeing her at all. He doesn't want to see her looking sloppy, shabby, messy and overworked every day, so he just doesn't *look* at her. He's afraid his faith in his own good judgment in marrying her in the first place will be destroyed.

These are, of course, fundamentals for keeping a man after you get him. Now let's talk about individual cases, about dressing to keep *your* man. You went through all that trouble to find out about him, what type he is, what he likes and dislikes, his hobbies, interests, pet peeves and weaknesses, before you married him. Don't throw that valuable information out the window the minute you leave the altar.

If you married the Sportsman, don't start nagging him to go to the movies when he wants to play golf or beg him to take you dancing when the World Series is on nighttime T.V.

If you won your conservative husband with your own quiet, well-mannered behavior and understated taste in dressing—don't change your entire personality once the ring's on your finger by buying wild beaded draperies, oriental hassocks and exotic modern carpets to furnish the love nest. If you do, he's likely to fly right into the arms of his secretary. You can bet she's conservative, because *he* picked her!

What you wear to keep that man happy and loving should be as carefully adhered to after marriage as before. With a home and children to care for, you can't always look as though you stepped out of a fashion advertisement, but you don't have to let him see you looking as though you were shot out of a cannon, either.

For your own self-preservation as well as his, take a little time to make yourself pretty before breakfast and before he comes home. Hair curlers belong hidden when he's around. Lipstick and a dab of perfume is as important as the breakfast eggs and bacon to prove you're really cooking. One fresh, well-pressed dress when he comes home will preserve your dignity and his affection longer than the huge mound of ironing you finished just as he walked in the door. Let some of it go until tomorrow, and get your own appearance ironed out instead.

Men, more than women, are the romanticists. While a woman remembers the roast lamb in the oven, a man forgets about everything except his Lamb. Men want more than food, more than sexual satisfaction, more than sleep. They want the delight, excitement and illusion of romantic love.

A man who doesn't have some romance at home is sure to look for it elsewhere. And what is romance in feminine form? It's any woman of any age whose husband thinks she's lovely to look at *in the morning*. If you make this your goal, you have the edge over the most glamorous women on earth. After all, he doesn't know how *they* look at 8 A.M.!

SUCCESS FORMULA FOR DRESSING TO GET AND KEEP A HUSBAND

1. Decide what kind of man you *want.*

2. Find out what kind of girls he likes.

3. Know what kind of fashions please him.

4. Don't masquerade in clothes that you hate just to attract a man. Be sure you are really, deep-down his type of girl. If you aren't—find another man.

5. Learn all you can about him, his hobbies, his interests, his likes and dislikes.

6. Be interested in his interests.

7. Choose your wardrobe to please him *and to suit his way of life.*

8. After you get him, stay the way you were, *and don't relax into a post-marriage slump of careless dressing.*

9. Look reasonably enticing in the morning—better at night.

3

How to Dress
YOUR FAMILY FOR
SUCCESS

3. How to Dress Your Family for Success

If you are married and a mother, your sense of the fitness of things will be judged not alone on what *you* wear, but on how your husband and your children look every day in the week as well as on Sundays. They mirror both your taste and your place in the community. They are reflections of how much you care, how neat you are, how dedicated you are to them and the kind of future you plan for them. The woman who is always elegantly coiffed, meticulously dressed and fashionably turned out while her mate and offspring look like orphans of the storm deserves, and gets, little credit for her sparkling appearance. Her selfish devotion to herself is likely to prove a boomerang by achieving the direct opposite of Dale Carnegie's famous goal of winning friends and influencing people.

Even the busiest of movie stars find time to assist their families in being better dressed. Greer Garson, Rosalind Russell, Elke Sommer and Anne Bancroft all help in the selection of their husbands' wardrobes. As for their children, Debbie Reynolds, Anne Baxter, Lucille Ball, Joanne Woodward and others too numerous to mention spend many happy hours shopping with their children and planning their wardrobes.

CLOTHES MAKE THE MAN

Closely hinged as the whole family is to your husband's progress, it behooves you to take special pains to see that he is not just dressed well, but that he is always dressed appropriately for the various activities that make up your life together and separately. Some wives devote great attention to what their husbands are going to wear to a party, but fail completely to show any interest in what their breadwinner wears to business. If you want not just butter but caviar on your bread, you'd better open your eyes to the fact that while clothes don't *make* the man, they do play an important part in boosting him up the ladder of success to recognition, respect and a higher income bracket.

Statistics prove that about eighty-five percent of all men's clothing purchased in the United States is either bought by or *influenced* by women. Whether or not you go out to buy your husband's shirts, socks, neckties, underwear and pajamas, your influence can make a big difference in how he looks. The man who looks good makes good faster than the man who is carelessly put together, badly pressed or poorly co-ordinated.

Husbands, of course, come in an assortment of sizes and shapes just like wives. And they also come with set dressing habits, often created long before you ever came into the picture. If you are one of those fortunate women with a real Dapper Dan for a husband, you don't have to worry much about his wardrobe. He's interested in clothes, assembles them carefully, collects them constantly and pays plenty of attention to their upkeep. With him your only worry is likely to be how you can keep up with him and stop him from spending the entire family clothing budget on himself.

If on the other hand your husband is inclined to be a Sloppy Joe, you have a problem on your hands. He hates dressing up and he really doesn't like clothes until they're so broken in they're broken down. Getting him to buy or wear anything new is as hard to accomplish as getting him to have a haircut. As the psychiatrists say, 'This guy needs help.' Getting him on the analyst's couch, however, is no solution. Getting him *off* the couch in the living room when he's wearing his best, freshly pressed suit is a recurring nightmare you have to face regularly.

The best way to handle this situation is to take the responsibility for

his wardrobe in your own hands. His apathy about clothes will stand you in good stead. He couldn't care less—so he'd rather have someone else take over. Keep a constant check on the condition of his clothes as he drops them with abandon around the house. See to it that they are pressed, have all their buttons and are spotlessly clean. When he's out of the house review his collection of suits, and then see what's in that bureau drawer to go with them. If the accessories (shirts, ties and socks) are completely lacking in co-ordination possibilities, get rid of them and start building replacements that go with the suits. If necessary, lay his clothes out each morning so you're sure things go together. Flatter him when he looks good, reminding him of how handsome he looks in certain colors. Buy him a valet stand on which clothes can be laid out easily and regularly. If he always forgets to have a shine buy him an electric shoeshiner and keep it where he can't help tripping over it in the morning. Get him a subscription to *Esquire*. Tell him you know he'll love the articles and stories. He won't be able to avoid the fashion features as he's going through each issue. Read it yourself and make suggestions for additions to his wardrobe. Over a period of time you'll see a change in your man. The metamorphosis from sloppy to snappy might not take place overnight, but you'll be starting new habits that will gradually replace the old.

Not all men fall into the two categories of Dapper Dans and Sloppy Joes. In between is the great, vast multitude of husbands who are just average when it comes to clothing concepts. They are neat. They want to look their best. They try. But somehow or other they just miss looking great for a lot of little reasons. Some of them have no sense of color at all. They'd as soon as not wear a green striped shirt with a blue suit and a red-and-blue-patterned necktie. They buy good suits, but fail to have them properly fitted because they just don't know what fitting can do to improve their own shapes. They're inclined to buy shirts with unflattering collars for their particular faces, and the fact that their shirt cuffs hang out too far from their jacket sleeves doesn't bother them a bit. It is very often some little defect in a man's wardrobe that keeps him from looking his sartorial best, and here again your wifely wisdom and loving care can go to work. If your husband's suits never seem to fit right, go with him when he buys the next one. Make sure the pants are the right length, that there is no bunch at the back of the jacket collar, that sleeves are properly altered, that the jacket doesn't gap across the middle when buttoned. Remember, alterations are free on men's clothing so there's no economy in poor fit. Through trial and error, find the best collar style for his face and neck. Does he look better with a medium-spread collar? A short tab? An oxford button-down? Longer points? Whatever shirt type does the most for him, stick with it and keep buying the same type.

Most women find themselves shopping fairly frequently for themselves, their children and their homes. My advice is always go into the men's departments when you are in a store. Look around at what's new in men's wear. If your husband's shirts never seem to fit him right, you will find that one manufacturer makes proportioned shirts in seventy-three different sizes to fit all types of men. If you don't like the colors and patterns your husband selects in suits or sports jackets, recommend something to him that you saw with your own eyes. The more you know about what's available, the more helpful advice you can pass on to the man in your life. You can tell him about the wonderful new textile marvels that are cropping up every day. Beguile him with the comfort of the new stretch fabrics, the easy care of permanent press, the wrinkle resistance of the lightwear polyester blends, the self-ironing shirt fabrics. Get him interested in technical advancements in order to make him think anew about men's fashions. While you don't want to turn Pop into a fop, you can do a great deal toward 'packaging' him better for his job, his leisure life, and as a proud escort for you.

In working out your campaign to improve your husband's appearance, use tact. Telling him he has bad taste, looks sloppy or that he dresses like a yokel will get you nowhere. Emphasizing his *good* points and suggesting ways he can capitalize on them will expand his ego. Telling him that a continental slimline suit makes him look taller is a lot better than saying he looks like a walking anthill in the one he's wearing. Mentioning the fact that a lower-cut shirt collar is very flattering to him will make him love you far more than telling him he has a fat neck.

Remember, just as you want your husband to look good to others, he wants most of all to look good to *you*. If your advice is given tenderly, lovingly and with genuine interest he will listen and be grateful.

FORMULA FOR HAVING A BETTER-DRESSED HUSBAND

1. Take an active interest in how your husband looks and in his wardrobe. Analyze both him and it.

2. Learn about men's fashions. Know about fabrics, styles, features and prices. Shop men's departments and men's magazines.

3. If your husband's wardrobe concept needs improvement, work with him (rather than on *him) to educate his tastes, change habits and turn his indifference into enthusiasm.*

4. Shop with him and for him to make sure his clothing is becoming, well-fitted, flattering and properly co-ordinated.

5. Most important of all, help to keep his wardrobe in condition— clean, pressed and mended. A well-groomed man looks *successful and has the best chance of* being *successful.*

DRESSING THE CHILDREN

There is little question that the expertise you develop in dressing both yourself and your husband will rub off to some extent on the children of the household, regardless of whether they are boys or girls, toddlers or teens. As the twig is bent so grows the tree, and the example set by yourself and your spouse in regard to wearables will, like your standards of behavior, table manners and other elements of proper upbringing, influence every apple-of-your-eye on the family tree.

Standards of dress for small children have been greatly simplified over the years. A glance backward at the overdressed Lord Fauntleroys, the beruffled and starched Mary Pickfords, the ante-bellum belles in hoop-skirts or the long stockings and high-buttoned shoes of the early 1900's make us realize how fortunate today's children are to live in an era when fashion and comfort go hand in hand.

Children of pre-school and nursery-school age, who haven't yet formed any clothes sense, are of course the easiest to dress. They have no choice in the matter of what to wear, and the decision is left entirely to Mother. With the possible exception of wanting to 'dress up' in costumes as Batman, astronauts and ballet dancers, the small fry simply conform to Mother's wishes. But this period, alas, is all too short-lived, for the minute they enter school they begin to have minds of their own about clothes. Girls are quicker to pick up the threads of fashion than boys, who prefer dressing themselves in layers of dirt, but this is the period (age five to twelve) when lifetime dressing habits will be formed. This is when the molding of children's ideas about clothes, their understanding of 'appropriate' dressing and their respect for their clothing should be inculcated.

They must be taught that there are different clothes for different

Family

purposes: that the beloved baseball suit belongs on the sandlot and not in the classroom, that the party dress is for parties, not bicycle riding, that blue jeans are for playtime, not dining out. If the fine points of dressing properly for the occasion are not pinpointed during these formative years, hard-to-break habits will be formed, and you're likely to wind up with an entire family of Sloppy Joes, whether your husband is one or not.

When your child—boy or girl—first goes off to school he is entering a brand-new world where he is not necessarily accepted without qualification as he is in the home. His teacher, as well as his classmates, will assess him in beady-eyed appraisal as he enters the classroom, and in large measure their impressions will stem from his outward appearance. If all the other boys are wearing Eton suits with collar and tie and your boy appears in a T-shirt and shorts, there's no question he (or you) will be viewed as an oddball. If your little girl checks into first grade wearing a velvet dress when all the others are in pleated skirts and sweaters, she's going to feel as though she has green hair. So don't take chances on how to dress them. Find out. Go to the school and wander around as the children come out for recess. Observe the 'going look' at that particular grade level, and dress your child to match it. Children not only perform better if they don't feel different from the others, but they'll be accepted faster by everyone.

Different schools have different rules—whether they are actually written down or not. In some areas the clothing requirements for school are extremely casual and in others they are more rigid. Some teachers insist that little boys wear shirts and ties, others don't. The only way to be sure is to do your own research on location the way we do at Paramount when we want to know what is worn in a specific area, in a specific industry or in a specific kind of environment for a specific film.

Outside of school, your child's wardrobe and dressing habits become a little more complex. This is where you have to separate the boys from the girls. Little boys tend to rail against ever getting 'dressed up.' 'Why can't I go to church in my sneakers?' 'Why do I have to change my clothes to meet Daddy at the office?' These are just a few of the never-ending questions mothers have to answer when it's suggested that Junior get cleaned up and change into a clean outfit. Conversely, little girls are so anxious to get dressed up that you have to hold them in check to keep them from overdoing it. They want to wear the new party dress to school. They will sneak out to play in the Sunday coat unless you watch them. They are naturally clothes-conscious and want to change their clothes as often as they change those of the fashion dolls they play with, from Barbie to Marge to Midge to Betsy McCall.

Frequently mothers tend to cast their girl children in pre-set roles and dress them to type. We've all seen mothers who think little Suzie is so feminine she should always wear ruffled panties, very short full skirts and curly hair regardless of where she's going. We've met others who insist their little daughters are real tomboys and confine them to wearing stretch pants and boy's shirts. These poor children play their parts like puppets on a string, while their mothers stifle any budding individuality they might develop. They are inhibited at an early age by the idea that they are different from other children, and all too often they grow up believing they are types when to others they are simply characters.

When you see a child inappropriately or badly dressed, remember it is rarely the child's fault—it is the mother's. And the chances are the mother will be just as tastelessly dressed too. Women who fool around elegant stores wearing tight pants and house shoes are likely to be dragging along a youngster in a swimsuit.

My plea to all mothers who know there is a difference between what to wear in the backyard and what to wear downtown is: dress your children as carefully as you dress yourself. The eight-year-old who is allowed into a hotel lobby in shorts and bare feet is being given a head start on becoming an eighteen-year-old offbeat beatnik.

Save the play clothes for the play areas, and when you take the children shopping, to restaurants, to shows and to visit, make them understand that these are 'special' occasions that call for 'special' clothes.

SUCCESS FORMULA FOR DRESSING
YOUNG CHILDREN

1. Research the dressing habits of the school your child will attend, and adhere to the 'look' that is established.

2. Teach your child the difference between play clothes, school clothes and dress-up clothes and explain how important it is to know which to wear when.

3. Select simple, easy-to-care-for clothing for all purposes. Let the child shine through. Never buy clothes that overpower the natural look of childhood.

4. Be sure your child is comfortable *in his or her clothes— both physically and environmentally.*

5. Teach your children the importance of good grooming and why people find neatly dressed children so appealing.

6. Dress your child as thoughtfully as you dress yourself.

"The herd instinct" - teenagers like to
dress alike regardless of size or shape!

Entirely different from other 'children,' teenagers (both male and female) *know* what they want to wear, and they get it—to the tune of clothing expenditures amounting to millions of dollars a year.

TEENAGERS MIX THEIR OWN

In spite of what many people think, teenagers have been fashion innovators for more than forty years. Back in the Twenties it was teenagers who first bobbed their hair, opened their galoshes (probably where the word 'flapper' came from), learned the Charleston and became members of an unorganized organization called the 'shifters.' A shifter wore a small brass paper clip as a club pin which signified that anything he or she wanted that was worn by another shifter could be asked for on sight, provided the asker had something to exchange (or shift) with the asked. In the Thirties it was again the teenager who first lengthened her skirts, roared around in rumble seats and danced the Big Apple. The post-war Forties, however, saw the teenage girl emerge on the scene as a 'special' fashion customer for the first time. This is when the Teen Departments came into being in the retail picture and a new fashion customer, with her own size range, market and budget, was born. In the Fifties and Sixties teens invented the sloppy look, were responsible for the biggest increase that ever hit bobby-sox sales, lindied their way to new prominence and followed through with the Kookie look, the Beat look, the Mod look, the Chelsea look, the Frug, the Frog, the Swim, the Surf, the Monkey, the Watusi and the What-nextie?

The point I want to make here is that from modest beginnings as the between-age ugly ducklings in the average family some forty years ago, the teenager has become a bellwether of fashion influence everywhere. In recent years they have actually been trend-setters for many fashions and enthusiasms adopted by adults, including clothing, dances, sports and art forms. The influence of the teenager on our society cannot be overlooked, and if you have one in your home you might as well get hip to what beats in his or her world, or you'll be slotted as a cube from nowhere.

Youngsters today begin to 'think teen' at about the age of eleven—getting themselves ready for the grand and glorious spree to come by demanding every new teen fashion that hits the market. Boys as well as girls get the bug at this age as any mother well knows who has been bugged to buy Beatle shirts, Beatle boots and to put up with Beatle haircuts. To resist all such demands and refuse to let the budding teenager indulge in some of these faddy passions is to place your youngster in the untenable position of not being in the same wave length with his contemporaries. The best you can hope to do with teenagers is to guide them to a more moderate path in their enthusiasms. Permit your thirteen-year-old son to have an 'intermediate' Beatle haircut rather than one that brushes his shoulders. Let your sixteen-year-old daughter wear her dress two inches above her knees, but not four. Give a little, take away a little. Make compromises with what means conformity to you—recognizing that teens want to conform too, but to *each other,* not to you.

Of all the ages of childhood, it is between twelve and eighteen that your offspring will be most interested in clothes. What to wear *where* is of vital concern to this group, and if your daughter insists on going to a dance in shorts and a zip-front surfing jacket, you can bet that is the 'going' garb at that dance. She *knows*—she has found out—and if all the girls are dressed that way and she appears in a dress, she'll be a wallflower, out of water, striking out faster than the batter of a flyball.

The sensitive teenagers, male or female, are very conscious of how their mothers look too. Your teenage son may dress like a beatnik but he doesn't want Mom going around looking Mod, mad or far out. If your daughter wears kookie clothes, don't try to look like her. She wants you to look smart, young and attractive, but not like one of *her* crowd. There's enough competition there already.

The teenage group is the sole area where dressing appropriately for the occasion requires a separate definition. For a teen, what might seem appropriate to you might be hopelessly inappropriate in the wonderful, wacky world in which she whirls. Here the question of what is right for the occasion cannot be answered by anyone but the individual teen who alone *knows* what will be worn by others at a particular function, whether it is a dance, a sleepover, a beach picnic, a barbecue or a football game. Forcing your ideas down the throats (or onto the backs) of your teenagers can make the difference between normal out-going kids and ingrown, introverted, in-the-house neurotics. So don't do it.

You may not like the things teenagers want and buy. You may rave and rant about what's become of the younger generation. But, Mom, you'd better face it, because you can't change it! It was ever thus from the Gibson Girl to the Bloomer Girl to the It Girl to the girl of today. So get with it yourself. Read *Seventeen* magazine and learn about teens from them. Recognize each current trend in fashion, and try to pick the best of that trend for your teenager, steering her gently away from the too far out but still keeping her on the in road that spells success with her crowd.

Really look at the friends your teenagers bring home. Do they look different from your offspring? Or do they all have a similar way of dressing? Isn't it true that if your child thinks a new fashion is cool, it's because the whole crowd is wearing it and to be without it is to be a cube? Don't judge teen tastes by your tastes.

Do some thinking back about your own teen years and remember what *your* mother went through trying to get you to conform to *her* way of thinking. Don't force issues; use gentle, sensible persuasion.

You might consider yourself successful if you get your teenagers to accept your taste, your ideas and your standards of dressing—but it could lead to utter failure at their level.

In spite of their intense interest in fashion and fashion fads, teenagers are apt to be herded into fashion without any regard for how they look. This is where you can really exert some influence without doing any harm.

Make a point of cleanliness on the basis of maintaining a clear, attractive skin. Set aside a special once-a-week good-grooming night when everyone shampoos, manicures and pedicures. Get Dad to work with the boys while you work with the girls toward this Operation Clean-up. Make cleaning the closet a simple routine the same evening, seeing to it that soiled clothes are sorted out for washing, cleaning and mending. Stress daintiness with the femmes, social acceptance with the boys.

And don't forget, the teenager remains a teenager for only a few years. After all, what parent could stand it much longer!

FORMULA FOR HELPING TEENAGERS
DRESS SUCCESSFULLY

1. Take an interest in their clothes, but don't try to change the trends they know are in.

2. Invite their friends over to convince yourself that that's the way they all look.

3. Make them responsible for the care of their clothes.

4. Steer them away from the way-out trends toward the moderate pathway of the in fashions they need to be part of their own set.

5. Emphasize good grooming and cleanliness in every way— by setting a good example yourself.

4

How to Build a
SUCCESSFUL
WARDROBE

4. How to Build a Successful Wardrobe

Since time began, women in all walks of life have had a single and continuing lament. Those with great wealth, as well as those living on limited budgets, have wailed to their poor henpecked spouses, 'I haven't a thing to wear.'

As far as I'm concerned, no woman in history has ever had a right to this complaint with the possible exception of Lady Godiva. If you are one of the many who find themselves frequently in this predicament, blame yourself, not your husband. Your failure to build a proper wardrobe for your own way of life is the only thing that brings you face to face with a function, an activity, a place or an invitation which your wardrobe cannot accommodate.

At the same time that most women claim they have 'nothing to wear,' they repeatedly grouse and groan about closet space. They have dozens of things hanging around that they *never* wear, either because they don't fit, are unbecoming or are inappropriate for the things they do and the places they go. If you are one of these Woebegone Winnies—here's some advice: take each of those hardly-ever-worn dresses, coats, suits and shoes out of hiding and make a decision. Are you *ever* going to wear them? Are they worth the money and effort to have them fixed up? If not, sell them—or give them to a poor needy relative. If all your relatives are rich, give them to the charwoman or the Salvation Army. You'll be doing a good deed for somebody else—and for yourself as well. Besides, your husband (or your mother, as the case may be) will be denied the exquisite satisfaction of saying, 'What do you mean you have nothing to wear? If you put one more thing in that overstuffed closet, the plaster will crack!'

Building a proper wardrobe is somewhat like building a home. Think of it like a home—because your wardrobe is something you're going to live in. It must be not only comfortable, but adequate for all your needs.

Only you can know the full demands your life and activities make on your wardrobe. This is an area which becomes your sole responsibility based on a calm, rational analysis of your life.

The size of your wardrobe, naturally, depends on the variety of your activities, the extent of your social life, where you live, what you do and where you go. For example, if you're an unmarried business girl living in a big city and your age is between twenty and thirty, it is obvious that your wardrobe would be vastly different from that of a housewife and mother of three who lives in the suburbs. You will require more date clothes, while she needs more casual outfits to drive back and forth to school, to attend neighborhood lunches and to do the marketing.

But whoever you are, whatever you do, wherever you live, when you build a home or a wardrobe, you start with a foundation. In this case we don't mean a girdle and bra, but the clothing other people see you in. The foundation of every wardrobe like that of a home consists of the brick and mortar items on which you can build.

(1) Every wardrobe should include a good-looking suit that is casual enough to wear in the country with a sweater, but not so casual that it would be out of place in town shopping or at the office, with a series of appropriate blouses or sweaters.

(2) Every wardrobe should include a 'costume'—that wonderfully versatile combination of dress with matching coat or jacket that can take you so many places that call for an 'important' look. The costume goes to P.T.A. meetings and matinees. It goes to church

on Sunday and to the Women's Club. It meets your husband in town for dinner and a movie, and it greets your rich Aunt Emma when she arrives at the airport from Paris.

(3)   Every wardrobe should include a simple black—or dark—dress that can grace a bridge table, a luncheon or be dressed up with accessories at cocktail hour.

These three 'foundation' costumes are essential in a well-dressed woman's wardrobe. They will take you more places, more of the time, than almost any others. From there on you build your wardrobe to fit your individual life and the lives of your friends.

CHART YOUR ACTIVITIES

An excellent way to approach the building of a wardrobe which is especially designed for *you* is to make a blueprint plan. I don't mean an actual architect's blueprint, but a pencil and paper chart of your activities with the clothing requirements they call for. There is nothing more foolhardy than to buy clothes without such a plan, and that kind of hit-or-miss spending can only result in an unbalanced wardrobe which takes you nowhere, and an unbalanced budget which drives your husband crazy.

As women, we all have certain weaknesses and are inclined to go for certain types of clothes whether we need them or not. I know a woman who can't resist pretty shoes, and her closet is full of them, but she has nothing suitable to wear with them. Other women adore fancy, frilly lingerie and fill their bureau drawers with lacy slips and nightgowns, but never have any money to buy outer clothing. One friend of mine, who has little need for dressy cocktail and evening clothes, is forever buying new ones. The result of this unfortunate indulgence is her startling appearance at the most casual gatherings all done up like a circus horse.

Conversely there are women so enamored of sports clothes that their closets are so bulging with tweeds, cashmeres, shorts, slacks and other rugged costumes that when they are invited to a dinner party or an afternoon bridge game they arrive looking as out of place as a belly dancer at a church social.

This is what a psychiatrist might call 'wish-fulfillment' buying. I won't venture into the subconscious desires of the woman who keeps buying all that fancy lingerie, or the foot fetish or Svengali syndrome of the Trilby with all those shoes, but I do know that yielding to such temptations results in what can only be called a 'sick' wardrobe.

In addition to satisfying you aesthetically your wardrobe must be functional. Fortunately, in these wonderful days where stores are filled with assortments of things for every occasion at all price levels in all size ranges, it is easy for Judy O'Grady and the Colonel's lady to combine function with fashion and be admirably dressed at all times. The woman who consistently makes errors in her choice of clothes in this age must be either stupid, careless or just plain neurotic. If she keeps buying the wrong things, winding up with a closet full of 'no-wears' it is my sincere hope that this chapter will help to set her straight. But if she continues to wander off the path I outline, gathering all the wild flowers of fashion rather than the durable perennials available, her closet will always look like a jungle, and she'll strangle in the overgrowth without even a decent fig leaf to wear.

Many *faux pas* of fashion can be avoided if you curb your instinctive desire to buy things with your heart instead of your head. If you hunger for certain types of clothes, for which you have little use, put yourself on a diet. Just as you resist too much whipped cream and French pastry to keep your figure in shape, you can say no to those yearned-for but unneeded purchases that lead to a wardrobe that is shapeless and without form.

Getting down to cases—*your* case, to be specific—here's how to start your blueprint. Just answer the questions in this list with one of the following words: every day, frequently, quite often, rarely, hardly ever.

How often do you:
  Go to business?
  Go to market?
  Go out dancing?
  Go to the theater?
  Go to informal dinners?
  Go to formal affairs?
  Go to picnics and backyard barbecues?
  Go to sporting events?
  Go on trips?
  Go to dinner in a restaurant?
  Go to bridge or card parties?
  Entertain at home?
  Go to school functions?
  Participate in church activities?

When you have answered these questions, it will be obvious to you where you should concentrate in building or remodeling your wardrobe. If you go marketing 'every day' and to sporting events 'frequently,' it is certain that you need a concentration of simple suits, sweaters, skirts and slacks, which can double in brass for both activities.

Wardrobe

INVENTORY YOUR WARDROBE

As soon as you've completed and checked over this list, adding any activities I've missed, take all the clothes out of your closet. Separate them into the categories on the questionnaire. How many costumes do you have that are right for business, for marketing, for dancing and so on? Lay them out in piles on your bed and on chairs. Do you have *enough* clothes for the activities you marked 'every day'? Do you have *too many* for those marked 'rarely' or 'hardly ever'? Does your wardrobe lean in one direction like the Tower of Pisa? Is it top-heavy with things you really don't need, and sparse in the areas marked 'frequently' and 'often'? Better start rebuilding, reorganizing and remodeling.

The appropriateness of what you wear has considerable bearing, too, on the community in which you live. Women who live in large metropolitan cities naturally need more sophisticated wardrobes than those who live in small rural towns where activities are centered around neighborly invitations and functions. The city-dweller might look perfectly elegant dining in a fabulous restaurant with a backless dress and a towering hairdo, but her country cousin in the same costume at the local inn would bring giggles to the lips of everyone present—and blushes to the hairline of her escort.

If you live in a small suburban community where social life centers around the country club, you need more changes than the city woman whose social circle is much larger. She doesn't see the same people at every party, but you do. You don't like to be seen over and over in the same old cocktail dress at the same old round of parties at the same old homes. Unless, of course, you look *simply great* in it. In that case the women may 'cat' about how many times you've worn it, but the men will just say, 'You never looked better,' as they try to steer you into a dark corner. A really terrific old dress that does something for you is far better than a brand new one that does nothing.

Conforming to the atmosphere in which you live is an important element of dressing for success. Success in any area involves having other people *like* you. Fundamentally, people don't like oddballs and freaks. They feel uncomfortable in the presence of people who are entirely different from them. When someone says of a woman, 'She's my kind of person,' that is the greatest compliment they can pay. If your way of dressing is completely out of keeping with your surroundings or with the tempo of life in your community, you're taking the chance of being classed with the weird ones, including the town drunk and the village idiot.

Many women have asked me if it is possible to have a well-built complete wardrobe on a limited budget. 'Money,' I tell them, 'is no guarantee of taste and the fitness of things, and an overstuffed closet is often as bare as a skeleton when it comes to *wearable* apparel.'

Those of us who have done any European travel have seen women disembark with a veritable train of luggage and spend hours going through customs. From my experience, these are frequently the women who have nothing to wear. On the other hand, the woman who manages to see all of Europe with just two suitcases has carefully planned her costumes to fit the place she is going and always looks right on every scene.

ACCESSORIES MAKE THE WOMAN

Accessories play a tremendously important part in building a wardrobe to live in. The woman who has all those shoes in her closet and nothing to wear with them is a prime example of bad planning. No one *needs* a pair of shoes for every costume, and a well-planned wardrobe is color co-ordinated so that one set of basic accessories (handbag, shoes and gloves) can be worn with a number of dresses or suits.

As far as basic accessories are concerned, if you had no others you could survive very nicely, and dress successfully for everything but the most formal occasions, with these:

Gloves:

Leather or fabric:	Shorties—dark, white or bone
	6- or 8-button—dark, white, beige or bone

Jewelry:

Pearls:	Single-strand
	Matinee-length necklace
	Earrings
Tailored Gold:	Necklace
	Button or drop earrings
	Bracelet
	One handsome pin or clip that can be
	worn on suits, dresses or coats
	(Preferably unmatching, so they go
	together but don't look like a 'set.')

Handbags and Shoes:	Black leather
	Beige or bone (Will go with everything.)
	Low-heeled sports shoe and tote bag in a
	neutral or luggage shade
	Medium-heeled conservative black dress
	shoes with matching leather bag

Frippery:	Several attractive scarfs to add color and
	dash to necklines or to wear on your
	head when necessary

Dressing appropriately for every occasion is one of the secrets of poise. A woman cannot possibly be at ease or at her charming best if she feels out of place because she's dressed inappropriately. There are very few women who like to be stared at. When all eyes seem to turn your way, it is time to start wondering whether your slip is showing, your eyelashes have slipped or your zipper opened, instead of considering yourself a ravishing beauty. The number of head-turning beauties around are few, but wearing the wrong thing for any occasion, and wearing it too short besides, can get plenty of stares for you, if you don't mind the snickers that go with them.

One of the prime rules of dressing appropriately is to be underdressed rather than overdressed, and we don't mean wearing next-to-nothing. We do mean stay on the safe side with simplicity. A movie star may be called upon to wear some very fancy get-ups to create the role she's involved in, but it's far better for your private life if you leave the glittering diamonds to Mae West, the sarongs to Dorothy Lamour, and the figure-fitting braless bias dresses to Carroll Baker. While the cinema has a decided influence on fashion trends (for example, the ruffled shirt from *Tom Jones*, the *My Fair Lady* hat, the bias-cut gowns from *Harlow*), they are usually redeveloped for popular consumption into far less flamboyant looks that are wearable by many women.

When, a few paragraphs back, I gave you some basic foundation items in both clothing and accessories to build your wardrobe around, you might have gotten the idea that I am recommending a uniform for every woman. This couldn't be farther from my intention. In the first place, these are merely *foundations to build on*. They are necessities, but if you don't build on them and around them you will have little more than a skeleton in your closet. According to your life and activities, you construct the rest of the wardrobe. If your social life is alive with sports-loving friends and you spend a lot of time at a country club, naturally your

wardrobe will concentrate on good spectator sports clothes. If you do a great deal of at-home entertaining, your closet should contain more easy hostess costumes than the woman who goes out to be entertained. If you are a business woman, the major part of your wardrobe will be developed around things that belong in the office. Decide what the *core* of your wardrobe should be.

YOUR SHOPPING GUIDE

Whatever your own wardrobe analysis reveals about your life and activities must be your shopping guide. When you list the clothes you now have according to the categories they fall into, you will readily see where your wardrobe is weak, where it is overdone and where it needs to be strengthened. But when you start the gradual job of remodeling it or rebuilding it, watch for and resist the shopping temptations nearly every woman falls prey to when she goes on a buying spree.

WATCH THOSE FADS

Keep aware of what's exciting and new in the fashion picture by reading the fashion magazines, but resist *short-lived fads or slavishness to fashion, unless you can afford to discard your entire wardrobe and buy a new one each season.*

When you buy a new coat or suit or dress, ask yourself whether the style you are selecting will look as good next year as it does this year. No matter what the current newest thing is, some styles age rapidly and are dated within a few months. There are others that are copied down into the low-end or cheaper market in no time, and like comets streaking across the sky, they make a wonderful display for a short time then die out overnight.

Rather than trying to catch the tail of every new fashion comet that streaks across the scene, hitch your fashion wagon to the steady stars that continue to shine on year after year. Fashion changes are never revolutionary, always evolutionary. There is a slow transition in silhouettes, rather than a sharp transformation. While fashion retailers try to make each new season seem like a complete change from the one before, the basic 'looks' change only by degrees over a long period of time. Most changes in fashion are a long time coming in and a long time going out, and the rule of thumb for complete change is known as the seven-year cycle. However, women who always buy the most extreme versions of each new fashion, rather than the moderate middle-of-the-road versions, are frequently stuck with a closet full of flash-in-the-pan fashions that wear out their news value in a single season, while the more conservative versions of the same costumes go on for years. In most cases the only change necessary to bring such clothes up to date is the hemline. And this, as you know, is the vital area in today's fashion look. Nothing is dowdier-looking than a skirt just a smidgen too long. As you review last year's wardrobe this year, try everything on—chances are last year's hemline is too long to be fashionable—or too short. This proves how important it is for girls to learn to sew. If I were President, I'd pass a law that every female in the United States would have to learn simple basic sewing, enough at least to change a hemline.

Every season there are new 'looks' aggressively featured by magazines and stores. Phrases like the 'London Look,' 'Total Look,' 'Sportive Look,' 'Mod Look,' 'Innocent Look,' 'Empire Look,' 'Darling Look,' 'Smock Look,' 'Elegant Look' or the 'Real Girl Look' are appearing daily to call your attention to clothes with a few outstanding different details which, in most cases, represent only a small portion of a store's stock. They receive a great deal of promotional emphasis because they are eye-catching. But if you examine the store's merchandise you will find that ready-to-wear buyers concentrate on fashions that have already proved their selling power and will be around for a long time. Examples are the Chanel suit with its youthful short jacket and braid trim, the shirtwaist dress with its simple button front and easy skirt, the shift with its unbelted away-from-the-body ease, the sheath with its gentle, figure-revealing body line, the A-line with its graceful swing, the straight slender coat with its youthful, weight-concealing slimness, and many others. These are fashions that have had a long life and still retain plenty of vitality. For the woman with a limited budget who cannot afford a completely new wardrobe every year, such conservative fashions represent good investments that pay long-term dividends. If you simply can't resist the urge to have something very, very new-looking, something entirely different, something really far out—indulge yourself with an inexpensive version, knowing that its life will be a short one. Better by far to make this purchase a dress because the investment involved in a coat or a suit will be greater, and a higher price tag calls for at least several season's wear.

How clothes feel, as well as look, is of tremendous importance. We have all seen women who seem inordinately self-conscious in their clothes. They pluck at the hem, yank at the sleeves, keep adjusting the neckline or are constantly checking themselves by looking in the mirror. Such women are not at home in their clothes because the clothes are not right for them. When you shop and try on something new in a store, consider this danger. Are those pretty sleeves (that look so wonderful in the fitting room) going to be a nuisance in the office? Are those fascinating big buttons going to be tiresome in a few weeks and make that dress too easily identifiable after a few wearings? Is that collar that rises high in the back going to feel as good under a coat as it does without one? Never buy clothes that overpower you and place you in a secondary role to what you're wearing. The right clothes for you are invariably those you feel right in, that you can put on and forget about, because they let your personality dominate them.

And don't think something's right for you because it looks so nice as you stand up before the fitting-room mirror, holding your stomach in. Move in it. Sit down. Cross your legs. Bend over. Walk. See if it rides up, wrinkles across the middle, or binds across the shoulders. Look at the back. Will it develop a seat-sag? Does it show your bulges? Will the belt pop open after dinner? Comfort and ease are essential to successful dressing. The most beautiful dress in the world is a pain in the neck if you can't be at ease when you wear it.

Another shopping danger that practically all women succumb to at times is the 'bargain.' No matter how big the markdown is, it doesn't represent a saving at all if the garment is going to be worn only by a hanger. How many times have you bought something just because you couldn't resist the fact that it was on sale for half its original price? Remind yourself that if it was such a desirable item to begin with, the retailer would never have marked it down. I admit that sometimes you will be fortunate enough to pick up a real gem at a reduced price—but don't buy it just because it's reduced. Ask yourself if you would have bought it at its full price. If not, forget it. You're better off spending a little more and having something you're really going to live in—and enjoy. Wearing the right thing at the right time is, I repeat, the key to successful dressing. *Having* the right thing in your closet for every occasion is just a matter of planning. Every item in your wardrobe should be there to serve a purpose, and if it just hangs there without ever going on your back you know it's as useless as a flashlight without batteries or a camera without film.

You might well take a tip from some of the stars on the organization of your closet. Julie Andrews, for instance, has her wardrobe arranged almost like stock in a department store. Each classification (day clothes, sports clothes, afternoon and evening clothes) is hung together and separated by a divider. Her accessories are labeled as to what they go with according to a master chart on the back of her closet door. Dressing in a hurry, she selects her costume, then refers to the chart and knows immediately which shoe, bag, hat, gloves and jewelry to wear with it. Debbie Reynolds has another method. Her closet door has a blackboard on the inside where she keeps a day-to-day list of things to be mended, altered, cleaned, put away or purchased. I've done this myself and find it a great joy to know not only what your closet contains, but what condition it is in at all times.

Movie stars who make personal appearances throughout the country are constantly faced with the problem of dressing right for a series of different occasions within a period of a few days. Joan Crawford recently made such a trip, and the first thing she did was analyze her schedule to find out not only where she'd be but what she had to do and what sort of people she'd be with. A talk to a group of university drama students indicated tailored clothes; acting as hostess at a charity bazaar called for a dressy afternoon dress; planting a tree at a ground-breaking breakfast made sports clothes essential. A talk at a women's club, an appearance on television, a gala dinner dance—each activity called for its own special just-right look. Yet Joan went on this trip with just *one* suitcase, plus a hatbox for the accessories she had carefully selected to complete and vary each costume.

There is nothing so destructive to a woman's charm as the dreadful feeling of being dressed wrong for an occasion. Standing out like a sore thumb is really more painful than a sore thumb ever could be—and trying to be your most gracious best in a situation where you feel as alien as a visitor from Mars is a nightmarish experience to any sensitive person. If you don't know what to wear for a given occasion, by all means ask someone who does know. If it's a party, ask your hostess. If you're making a speech, ask the committee chairman. If it's a wedding, ask the bride whether it's formal or informal. People love to be asked for advice. It

makes them feel important. So don't spare the questions if you are in doubt.

In building your wardrobe, it is also important to decide each season what your color schemes are going to be. If you buy a lot of scrambled colors that bear no relation to each other you're going to be in trouble with accessories. Choose a few becoming colors and build your wardrobe around them instead of getting on your clothes horse and galloping in all directions. Your color sense should be tempered by common sense as well as your own complexion. You'll find some guidance on this score in Chapter 7.

FORMULA FOR BUILDING A SUCCESSFUL WARDROBE

1. Make a blueprint of your activities.

2. Check your entire wardrobe to see if it fits the blueprint of your life and activities.

3. Be sure your closet contains the foundation items you wear most often.

4. Build soundly on this basis by buying to a plan that is right for your life.

5. Don't get carried away by the latest craze or the biggest bargains, particularly if they don't fit into your plan.

6. Think in terms of a livable wardrobe—one that is not only aesthetically pleasant, but one that works for you, that you feel good in and that makes you look right in every situation.

5

How to Succeed
IN LOOKING
YOUNGER

5. How to Succeed in Looking Younger

Youth is the keynote of the age we live in, and it has become the greatest selling force in the merchandising of everything a woman wears or uses. Magazines and newspaper advertisements dramatically feature the youthful figure today's bras and girdles can create, the younger skin made possible with a multitude of creams and lotions or the age-defying results of various hair-coloring products. It is no longer important how young you are; it is how young you look that counts. Growing old gracefully used to begin at about thirty-five, but today few women think in those terms. They prefer to 'stay young, gratefully' with thanks and praises to the designers, the beauticians, the dieticians, the exercisers and even the plastic surgeons who help them look younger than they are from the minute they are old enough to start snipping a few years off their age.

Not too many years ago clothes were categorized by age. There were 'women's' dresses and 'Mama' hats for females who no longer felt comfortable shopping in a misses' department. Today women of all ages buy 'junior' clothes if their figures permit. 'Juniors' in retail parlance are referred to as a size, not an age. And most big department stores and specialty shops place the accent on youth in their moderate-priced sections by calling them names like 'The Debutante Shops' and 'The Young Circle' with only one thought in mind. Not to keep the older woman *out*, but to entice her in—because any woman young enough to walk would rather walk into an area where clothes are young and zippy than into a morgue-like shop devoted to 'older women.'

As medical science has worked to keep people alive longer, old age itself has been pushed further up the numerical scale. Middle age used to start around thirty-five, now it begins somewhere between forty-five and sixty, depending on the individual's viewpoint and how the individual looks.

Some of the fabulous grandmothers in movieland can be an inspiration to many women ready to give up the ghost as far as looking young is concerned. If you feel creaky, look old and think you've just about had it, take a look at Marlene Dietrich, Gloria Swanson, Joan Crawford, Bette Davis and a host of other movie stars none of whom are under fifty, but who look vital, beautiful and years younger than they are.

How do they do it? They take excellent care of their skin, hair and figures, of course. These are things every woman should do as a natural precaution for preserving youth at any age. But the real foundation of youth today is the wealth of young, wearable fashions available to women in every economic stratum. Mothers no longer retire to the background when their daughters reach maturity. The clothes they wear have just as much youthful verve, color and fashion news as the next generation's and sometimes more. The young ones are inclined to go for fads, exaggerated trends and anything far out—while the mature woman who looks younger than her years steers away from the 'Mod,' the 'Pop' and the 'Op' for the moderate, the flattering and the opposite of flaming youth.

There is serenity but not severity in the clothes she selects. Her daughter might choose a mad, exotic print that dazzles the eye and addles the mind, but she picks a cooler, more flattering, feminine print that softens her look.

As the years advance, the right clothes are the greatest ally a woman has in camouflaging the signs of age that are as inevitable as autumn leaves at summer's end.

The accent on youth in America is so strong that the mature or middle-aged woman is almost entirely forgotten by the great retail establishments throughout the country. While clothes for the mature woman are available everywhere, the emphasis placed on them in advertising and window displays is practically nil. Perhaps the reason for this is a kind of retail-oriented ruse to make every woman forget that time marches on and that what is sauce for the gosling is fine for the goose too. Or is it because so many retail establishments are run by men who have been so impressed with the statistic that more than twenty-five percent of our population are now under twenty-five that they forget that thirty-five percent are over forty? I don't know the reason why stores fail to beckon to, entice and glorify the middle years of womanhood or why fashion magazines devote so little space to clothes for women over forty, but one of these days I feel they will wake up to the tremendous profit potential in this affluent, eager market.

The older woman is a major source of revenue in every fashion area. She is the woman who has invariably 'arrived' as far as income is concerned. Her husband is at the peak of his earning power. Her children are grown or nearly so, and she has more time, and money, to spend on herself. She can afford higher-priced clothes than the little secretary on the way up. Her social activities are more numerous and her position in the community calls for a bigger and better wardrobe. Yet when you read the fashion press and the local newspaper advertisements all the appeals are made to the 'young elegants,' the 'young arrogants,' the 'young marrieds' or the 'young homemakers,' most of whom really haven't reached the stage in life where their nest eggs are hatching out *extra spendable dollars*. The young ones, in many cases, are still involved in paying for the TV set, the Hollywood bed, the nursery furniture, the car and the mortgage.

In spite of the over emphasis placed on fashions and furnishings for the young in most advertising and publicity, there is no lack of attractive merchandise for the older woman to buy. Depending on her figure, she is free to buy whatever she pleases whether it is designed for juniors, misses, petites, half-sizes or women. The size ranges produced by garment manufacturers range all the way from size three to size forty-eight so there is no need for the lady of uncertain years to look neglected even if she is somewhat overlooked in today's monumental and continuous appeal to youth.

A desire to look younger than you are (within the limits of good sense) is certainly no crime against society. If you manage at fifty to look somewhere between forty and forty-five, hooray for you. We have seen women look five, even ten years younger than their true ages—but only in the cases where major surgery came to the rescue have we ever seen a woman take off twenty years with success.

THE THREE C'S SYSTEM

A youthful spirit and good health are the greatest contributors to staying and looking younger than you are. Second only to these is dressing yourself adroitly, using what I call the 'Three C's System' (Cover-up, Conceal, Camouflage) which can cancel out quite a few years for almost any woman who has just reached thirty-nine, forty-nine, or fifty-nine for the third time.

The friendliest advice we can give you on this score really came from the lips of lovely Austrian-born Lilli Palmer, who said, 'Don't pick clothes so young that you wind up looking like mutton dressed as lamb.'

Maturity is a time for simplification of your clothing rather than flamboyance. Ruffles, sequins, bold overall prints, way out colors, too-high heels, plunging decolletages, tight pants and bikinis should be banished from your wardrobe because they are in most cases dead giveaways when worn by those of us who have reached what I prefer to call the 'interesting age.'

You've surely heard it said of some young person that no matter what she wears, she looks wonderful. The ebullience and healthy glow of youth is in itself a thing of beauty. But when some of your youthful loveliness begins to fade, when the tender dewy skin, the sparkling eyes, the shining wind-tossed hair start to look old and dull and messy, that's when a woman must spend more time, energy and effort on a wardrobe that aids her battle with age. She has to watch her necklines and necklaces when her neck begins to weather. She has to keep her eye on sleeve-lines when her upper arms get flabby.

She must avoid horizontal stripes and wide belts when her middle begins to thicken. She becomes, if she is smart, much more cautious in her buying of clothes, for she realizes she has reached the age where, no matter how girlish she feels at heart, she will only find the secret of youth in the sometimes chilling Fountain of Truth.

We have all known women who fail to see themselves as ever becoming mature or matronly. They refuse to wear glasses when they can hardly see. (Without glasses they don't see those crow's feet or added chins, either.) They continue to buy giddy, girlish clothes that exaggerate their age. They equate youth with such superficialities of fashion as short skirts, tight pants, wacky hairdos and wild eye make-up.

Looking younger than you are, without making youth a fetish or yourself a freak, is a fairly simple matter if you just look at your face (with your glasses on) in the cold, truthful daylight with a magnifying mirror. How old does your skin look? Your hair? Your eyes? Your mouth? Something can be done about all of them. They can be improved with care, creams, foundation make-up, tints, bleaches. The magic of today's cosmeticians and hair stylists is available to every woman.

A shorter, rather than longer, haircut gives an uplifting effect to sagging face lines. Bangs or soft wisps of hair over the forehead conceal some of those forehead creases. Deftly applied make-up plus eye-drops and enough sleep can do wonders for little tell-tale lines or larger tattletale bags around the eyes. Hair coloring in soft, natural tones will bring back glint and shine to faded graying hair. There are literally endless lengths to which you can go to make your face look younger, but wearing the wrong clothes will give your age away faster than your best girl friend.

That magic mirror in the fairy tale that kept telling the wicked witch that she was the 'fairest of them all' whenever she asked it might have been a handy gadget to bolster *her* feeling of insecurity, but a far handier tool for you, once you've turned thirty-five, is a truthful appraisal of your own assets and liabilities. How does your balance sheet look right now, and what are you doing to turn the gradual loss of youth into a rewarding success in maturity?

Let's start at the top with necklines. When you reach the age where your neck is beginning to look more like a hen's than a swan's, avoid little round collarless necklines unless you wear them with jewelry that falls *below* the neckline. Dog collars and choker necklines that draw attention to those folds, lines and blemishes should be avoided like skirts that show the knobs in your knees. If you sometimes think that your neck is getting *shorter* with the years, the chances are it's because your chin is getting *bigger*. Even thin women tend to develop a heavier chin line with the years. This is a signal to keep away from turtle-necks and high oriental collars which have a tendency to make you look as though you have no neck at all. The most flattering necklines to women no longer in the blush of youth are those that stay away from the neck. V-necklines, soft cowls and stand-away collars are excellent. They have a tendency to make necks look longer, chins smaller and to frame the face without focusing attention on the neck itself. Matinee-length necklaces and pendants, for the same reason, are far better than base-of-the-neck jewelry unless your neck is still something you want everyone to notice.

Very décolleté necklines should be avoided. If the skin on your neck and upper chest is still lovely to look at, wear them. If not, consider the softening influence of a pretty scarf (chiffon is a great flatterer) in a color that blends with the costume and does things for your eyes.

Your bustline, as the years roll on, may lack the small, round firmness of yesterday, but with today's ingenious shape-makers to guide you, there's no reason to have anyone realize it. (There are even pretty bras to wear to bed.) The selection of a bra, however, is as important as what goes over it. If your figure is full, don't squeeze it into a small bandeau which just pushes that extra flesh up and over, and don't pull your bust so close together that you're up to your chin in cleavage.

No matter how many years a woman drops from her age verbally, her elbows and upper arms can give her away visually. If you are one of the lucky ones whose athletic pursuits have kept your arms firm and youthful, and whose careful creaming has retained elbows soft and dimpling, go sleeveless, strapless, haltered or even topless. But if like many women past thirty-five (and most past forty) you are armed with sagging muscles or have elbows with 'elephant' skin, try some of these disarming ideas.

Never ever buy a sleeveless dress unless it has a jacket, stole, capelet or other cover-up feature. If your elbows are okay, but your upper arms aren't, you can frequently fix up the sleeveless dress you just can't resist by asking the store to get some extra material from the manufacturer and having small cap sleeves made. With formal evening clothes which are invariably bare at the top, the graceful above-elbow glove is a godsend for concealing ugly elbows, and an ethereal stole of tulle to match your formal dress will do as much for you (and your arms) as a soft-focus camera does for some movie stars' faces.

As the years roll on, it is likely that your midriff will roll on some extra bulk. Few women who had twenty-five inch waistlines in girlhood still boast the same measurements in their later years. Good foundation garments, well-fitted, can trim down and smooth out the bulges, but they cannot change the circumference to any great extent. What goes *over* your undergarments creates the final illusion of slenderness and makes you look as though you have a dearth of girth.

All of us have had the pleasant experience of meeting an old friend for the first time in several years and hearing those precious words, 'You look wonderful, you've lost weight!' Having just that morning tipped the scales at five pounds over our last high, we know it must be the dress we're wearing, which becomes the most favored object in our closet.

Chances are it was a body-conscious but easy-fitting dress—one of the greatest little waistline-concealers ever devised. But this is not the only fashion line open to the waistline-worried. The high-busted Empire silhouette is excellent too, if your bosom has remained small and firm. The long-waisted overblouse, the jacket costume and suits are other fine answers to the inevitable problem of midriff spread, and so is the fashion for straight-line dresses with hemline interest.

THE BIG DONT'S

The big *dont's* in this area are obvious: *Don't* wear wide, wide belts around your middle. *Don't* wear tied sashes. *Don't* wear blouses that terminate at the waist. *Don't* wear tight-fitting clothes of any kind. *Don't* go without a good girdle or all-in-one.

Skirt hemlines have become a growing problem in recent years for the woman whose years are advancing. Wearing her skirts the same above-the-knee length as her teenage daughter never took a single year off this woman's age. Even the most beautiful legs—Marlene Dietrich's for instance—look better when the kneecap is covered. It is obvious that if your legs are among your least attractive attributes, you cannot fly in the face of fashion by wearing skirts to your ankles, but common sense can guide you to the best length for *you*.

Skirts with hemline interest—pleats, ruffles or flounces—should be worn only by women with pretty legs, regardless of their age.

To improve the look of too-heavy legs, darker hosiery colors are splendid, while bold textured stockings are completely out for the heavy leg. They make wonderful camouflage, however, for legs with blemishes and veins.

Now, with your feet on the ground, let's talk about shoes. Many women have foot troubles as they grow older. Protruding joints, corns, calluses and ingrown toenails are never pretty sights to observe, nor are those red, spur-like pump-bumps at the back of the heel. Take a good look at your feet to determine whether they add or subtract from your age-image. If they are in the minus column, for Hermes' sake don't wear open-strapped sandals, sling-backs or go barefooted. Today's shoe fashions are so diversified, any woman can find footwear that is flattering and comfortable to both her feet and her age. The fashion for 'little' heels has made many feet look and feel younger. A footsore middle-aged female tottering around on high spike heels is a sad sight, and the way her feet feel invariably shows up in the sad-sack expression on her face. Today there are no longer any 'Mama' shoes. Even 'comfort' shoes have been styled up so that no one knows they are on problem feet. One leading manufacturer of such shoes now advertises 'Women have changed and so have Enna Jetticks,' showing a picture of two pairs of feminine feet. One wears the old-fashioned, broad-heeled black brogues that were once the badge of age, the other wears smart, fashionable pumps that are ageless.

Youth, like Beauty, is in the eye of the beholder. There is no reason on earth why a woman should not do everything possible to make herself look younger than she is, still bearing in mind the age recorded in the family Bible. 'Act your age' is still an excellent admonition to frugging grandmothers and pony-tailed forty-year-olds, but 'Dress your age *downward*' to the number of years you can get away with, *believably*, is our advice to every woman, everywhere.

Color plays a very important part in painting a younger picture of *you*. Soft-focus colors rather than harsh brilliant ones are kindest to mature complexions. A pale pink hat or blouse casting its rosy glow on your face will make you look younger than a brilliant one. Vivid oranges, electric blues and sharp greens are trying colors for all but the most flawless young skins and should be avoided except as accents. Warm beiges with a pink rather than yellow base are flattering to almost all skins, and navy blue is an ever-young color that can be relied on to put the You in Youth. Grays of the flannel or oxford family are basics for all ages and particularly young-making. Specific colors for you and your type are covered in another chapter, but if your cry is 'Color me young,' try some of the suggestions made here and see what a difference (in age) color can make.

As you grow older, it is natural that many things should change. Your step may lose some of its bounce, your body some of its suppleness and your face some of its freshness, but if you look at your friends and con-temporaries, you will be consoled by the truth that you are not alone. At the same time, among your own group, you will doubtless be struck by the fact that some of your friends look much younger than others. These are invariably the women who realize that the older they get the more time they have to spend on repairs. Neglect will not ravage a teenager's beauty, unless it goes on for a long time. But neglect in middle age will accelerate deterioration of your looks with a speed that is horrifying. Too many parties, too many martinis, too strenuous sports, too little sleep, too much rich food, too much *anything* is your enemy. If your social life is active, pace it. Have a night to catch up on sleep, beauty care and diet in between your social obligations. Allot enough time in your schedule to the details of fastidiousness that add so much to the success of looking younger. The 'who cares' attitude toward fingernails, toenails, depilatories, underclothing, hair and figure is a dangerous sign that can be detected in too many women once they have given in to the aging process. Yet of all the times in a woman's life when she needs to be metic-ulous about her looks, this is it.

Starting to compensate for the loss of youth by overindulgence in food, drink or harder work, will not only age you earlier, but shorten your life span. Maturity is the time to *act* mature and *think* maturely while you manage to *look younger.*

FORMULA FOR DRESSING TO LOOK YOUNGER

1. Steer away from extremes in everything and pick the middle-of-the-road fashions suitable to the age you can reasonably expect to look.

2. Analyze your physical assets and liabilities. Capitalize on the assets. Overcome the liabilities through the 'Three C's System' (Cover-up, Conceal, Camouflage).

3. Be fastidious about your clothing and yourself.

4. Avoid too-youthful, faddy fashions that make you look like 'mutton dressed as lamb.'

5. Be aware of the danger areas where age shows up first, and choose clothes that subdue rather than spotlight them.

6. Remember that good health and a happy spirit can take years off your age—and the right clothing can keep them off.

6

How to
ANALYZE YOUR FIGURE

6. How to Analyze Your Figure

One of the few fallacious quotations ever attributed to our beloved and revered forefather Benjamin Franklin was, 'With a pillow over their heads all women look alike.' Knowing women's figures as I do, I would have to tell dear old Ben to go fly his kite. If he were alive today, I'd take him into my designing room where stand hundreds of white cotton and fabric torsos which are replicas of the figures of famous movie stars whose wardrobes I create. There is no such thing as a standard size movie star, or woman for that matter. Identical measurements rarely occur even in identical twins. The cloth dummies in my designing room are as varied in contour, size, dimension and silhouette as the trees in the forest. Some are tall and willowy, others short and petite. Some have fullness at the top, others tend to widen at the bottom. Clothes have to be designed to camouflage their defects and exaggerate their assets. In different cases the object of a costume is to create height, to diminish width, to lengthen the leg line, to shorten the neck, to straighten a sway-back, to conceal a hint of tummy. Designing for women of many types requires, of course, a basic knowledge of current fashion trends and influences—but it means never, ever, being a slave to them, because it is far more important to make a woman look *better* than to make her look up-to-the-minute.

Remember, it is *always* fashionable to look your best. If all the fashion magazines are featuring horizontal stripes and you're five feet tall and wear size sixteen, it's far better to stick to solid colors than to go around looking like a Hula Hoop in motion.

The forest of torsos in my workroom proves that there are as many 'types' of women under contract in Hollywood as there are in the super-markets of Paducah or the subways in New York. The rounded curves of

Elizabeth Taylor look very different from the fashion-mannequin proportions of Audrey Hepburn. The size-five measurements of Debbie Reynolds are a very striking contrast to the voluptuous silhouette of Sophia Loren. Jane Russell could never be confused with Grace Kelly, nor could Mae West be considered a double for Natalie Wood. Before designing a wardrobe for any of these stars, the first step is the analysis of her figure.

As you know, everything is exaggerated on film. If an actress is inclined to be busty, her torso looks even more so on the screen. If she is hippy or bony or bow-legged or knock-kneed (oh, yes, even the stars have problems), these bodiosyncrasies are further amplified in photography. So each figure requires a special, individual diagnosis. And so does yours.

A DO-IT-YOURSELF ANALYSIS

How do you analyze your figure? Few women can go to the trouble and expense of having a specially molded torso made, but there is a do-it-yourself method that works just as effectively. First, put on a skintight-fitting figure-revealing undergarment or bathing suit, and decapitate yourself. Simply put a bag over your head with eyeholes cut out and look at yourself in the mirror. Minus a head, you're looking at your torso without the personality, sparkle, familiar understanding and natural self-esteem your own face, eyes and smile can add to the picture. Look at yourself from all angles and decide what kind of shape you're in, plus what figure type you are. Without this knowledge it is impossible to know what you should do about your figure, or what kind of clothes you should wear to make a success of looking better, slimmer, rounder, taller, smaller, more glamorous.

As you look in the mirror at this headless version of yourself, ask yourself (and answer honestly) what kind of body you see. Is it thick or thin? Is it straight or curved? Do the arms look too fat or too thin? How about the legs? Are they straight 'little-girl' legs, long shapely 'model's' legs, or the kind you'd rather not mention? Is the silhouette-line carved in at the waistline, or is there a bulge around the middle? Does the tummy stick out? Is the neck too thick, too short, too skinny, too long? What about the bust? Does it need to be lifted a bit? Padded a bit? Flattened a bit? Controlled?

Turn sideways and look at the profile. How straight is the back? Would a straight string hung from your head to the floor touch the back of your head, your shoulder blades and your buttocks or would it weave in and out like the map of West Virginia? Is this figure round-shouldered, sway-backed, derrière-droopy?

After you've gotten over the shock of these two views, take a hand mirror and stand with your back to the mirror to see how you look to others when you walk out of a room. Are your shoulders narrower than your hips? Do you have a hump from bad posture? Do you see angel's wings, lumpy hips? How do the backs of your knees look? Should you show them in public?

After you've made this experiment, if you feel perfectly satisfied with everything you see, we recommend you have your vision checked, because such perfection only exists in dreams or romantic sculptures.

The great diversity in the female form is attested to by what has happened over the years in 'standard sizes' of ready-to-wear. Where once there were only misses and women's sizes there are now petite sizes for the woman 5'3" and under, junior sizes, junior petites, teen sizes, half-sizes and tall girl sizes. Because even all these aren't sufficient, there are proportioned sizes in pants, skirts, hosiery and blouses.

Even the most looked at feminine figures vary in proportion in various parts of the country, a fact brought out when the Playboy Clubs opened up in Chicago, Miami, New Orleans, New York and other cities.

The key figure in these key clubs is the Bunny, official name for the exotic handmaidens (you just can't call them waitresses) who welcome and serve the customers and take those photographs that are proudly shown off back home or furtively destroyed as incriminating evidence.

A Bunny can't look like an ordinary mortal—and she doesn't. Every Bunny is custom-fitted with rabbit ears and a thigh-high satin costume that combines all the best —and I mean the best—features of a glamorous corset and a brief swimsuit. Well, in fitting these outfits some very interesting figures have come to light, in more ways than one.

It was soon discovered that Miami Bunnies are tiny, averaging size eight and wearing a B-cup bra. Chicago Bunnies have the biggest derrières of those yet covered by the Clubs, and New Orleans Bunnies wear C-cup bras and are big all over.

Regardless of the shape you're in or your basic figure type, the chances are the first step in analyzing your figure with your head in a bag will offer some surprises—both pleasant and disappointing. This information will come in very handy, so write it down under simple headings, with your honest appraisal of each part of your body.

Here's how the analysis of one famous star came out:

	Assets	*Liabilities*	*Action to be Taken*
Neck		Too short	Avoid high collars
Shoulders		Slightly rounded	Work on improved posture
Bust	Good		Choose clothes that show it off
Waistline	Just right		Don't hide it, belt it
Hips	Perfect		Wonderful for overblouses
Thighs		Somewhat bulgy	Avoid tight skirts, pants
Legs	Excellent		Wear skirts to mid-knee
Tummy		Protrudes	Exercise, diet, more control in girdle
Diaphragm		Flabby	Avoid tight bodices

After you've made this part of your analysis, keep the pencil handy and write down all your measurements, including your weight and height. Don't cheat by pulling the tape measure too tight. This record will be your guide in checking the progress you make in trying to move some of your liabilities into the asset column through exercise, diet and posture improvement.

A MAP OF YOURSELF

The second part of *Research Project You* requires an accomplice. Tape a large piece of wrapping paper to the wall and have your companion make a map of your figure on this paper with a heavy crayon or grease pencil, wearing the same figure-revealing costume as in the head-in-the-bag test (see illustration p. 100). Stand away from the outline and really study it. The measurements you have already recorded and the facts revealed by looking at yourself with the bag over your head will give you the opportunity to make an unbiased appraisal of your figure type, silhouette and proportions without any fantasies about how you *wish* you look. This is *you* in outline.

Psychoanalysis takes place on a couch with a doctor writing down your thoughts in the hope you'll get to know yourself and allay your anxieties. What we're talking about might be called physioanalysis. You do it standing up, but what you write down helps you to know your figure and get rid of any illusions you might have about it. Frankly I think this sort of analysis can in many cases eliminate anxieties and fears too, and any woman who doesn't find out all the facts about her own figure ought to go to a psychiatrist and have her head examined.

Now that you have taken a good long look at your length, width, proportions and measurements—consider that outline map of yourself. The map is a guide to where you are going. If you use it properly you will get where you want to go. If you ignore it, you're lost. The most important thing it will tell you is which one of these nine figure types you are:

1. Are you *Average*—in every regard?
   This means average height (between 5'2" and 5'6") and average weight for that height (between 112 and 127) depending on your bone structure. You are neither too fat nor too thin.

2. Are you average height, but overweight?
3. Average height, but underweight?
4. Are you tall (between 5'6" and 5'10") but exactly the right weight for your height?
5. Are you tall, but overweight?
6. Tall, but underweight?
7. Are you short (under 5'2") with poundage perfect for your height?
8. Short and underweight?
9. Short and overweight?

Check the category you fall into and then turn to Chapter 8 for some helpful recommendations on what to wear. Every woman's figure varies to some extent, but at the studio I have worked out this basic silhouette and color-value chart to help analyzed figures look better in clothes. These are basic recommendations, remember, and to use them properly you must take into consideration all the things you've learned about your figure in your physioanalysis. If you're 5'2" but very long-waisted, the chances are you cannot wear petite sizes even though the skirt length would be right for you. If you are narrow-shouldered but broad-hipped, one-piece dresses may present a size problem and separates may be your only solution.

IT MUST FIT

Variations in the feminine form are legion, and in buying ready-made clothes very few women can walk out of the store without some alterations. Excellent fit is one of the first requirements of dressing for success. Without it even the most elegant clothes look like something whipped up by loving hands at home. With it a budget wardrobe can take on the look of custom-made perfection. There is no question about the improvements good alterations can make in the way your figure looks in clothes.

A garment that is fitted to your figure, taking into consideration its deviations from perfection, can do a great deal to accent your assets and conceal your liabilities. Ill-fitting shoulders, gaps at the back of a neckline, side-seams that are strained even slightly or skirts that ride up when you're seated not only hasten the obsolesence of clothes, but will make them look like something handed down or borrowed from a friend of another size.

When you buy a dress don't look just at the length to see if it fits. Look at the neckline, the waistline, the hips and the shoulders. Does everything hit you at the right places or does it sag, bag, pinch and strain at certain points? Sit down in it. Is the skirt so tight that you're going to have a permanent 'seat' in it after the first wearing? Does the skirt ride up to embarrassing heights when you step into a car or a bus? Raise your arms to see if you will be able to dance or reach up to comb your hair

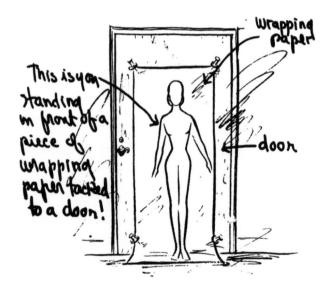

This is you side view →

Wear something tight fitting

Here I am showing how to outline your figure

Thumb tack a piece of wrapping paper to a door —

Wear something tight!

Here I am showing you how to have some one outline your figure without restraint. Move around in the dress before you buy it, and if you're not completely comfortable *walk away*, unless it can be fixed without an astronomical alteration bill.

When I fit an actress I make her go through an almost calisthenic routine—walking, jumping, lying down, sitting on the floor—not only to see if she can do these things comfortably but to see how the costume looks in action. None of us are store dummies. We are constantly on the move in business, in the home and in our social lives. Clothes that only look good when you stand still are for posing in, not for living in.

One day when I was involved in a fitting for Bette Davis, she suddenly leaped across the room, threw herself across a divan, then rolled off limp onto the floor. For a moment I thought I had stabbed her in a vital spot with a pin. She picked herself up, laughing, and said, 'Don't worry, I'm not losing my mind. That's part of the action in the scene I'm playing in this dress. I wanted to make sure I could work in it without feeling inhibited.' In one scene in *Torn Curtain* Julie Andrews had to jump on and off a bicycle, so we had a bike right in the fitting room so she could practice to be sure her clothes 'worked.'

Choosing the right type of clothing to achieve a desired result has been successfully accomplished in motion pictures for many years. Seeing such stars as Clara Bow, Gloria Swanson and Mae West on the screen, few moviegoers ever suspected their diminutive size (around five feet tall). The clothes that were designed for them created an impression of height. Unbroken close-to-the-body lines lengthen the silhouette and stretch out the figure. Stars who look like fashion models, for example, Audrey Hepburn, Roz Russell, Vanessa Redgrave and Lauren Bacall, try to achieve an opposite effect when their roles call for a petite small-girl look. Their tall 'model' figures are cut down visually by costumes that use two-piece effects, two-color treatments and broken lines that shorten the body.

You may not have the most perfect figure in the world, but there's no reason why you can't have excellent posture. Standing and sitting straight, holding in your abdomen and throwing back your shoulders, rather than letting your body fold up like a venetian blind, will do a great deal for the clothes you wear. Gloria Swanson is an excellent example of what proud posture can achieve even for a tiny woman. When she came back to the studio some years ago to make *Sunset Boulevard* I asked her if she ever minded being so tiny. She flashed her brilliant smile and told me, 'Not at all, Edith, because I never think of myself as small. I *think tall*.'

Thinking tall is a wonderful state of mind for women of any size, because the mental process involved straightens up their spines, lifts their chins, squares their shoulders and flattens their tummies.

You may think that a very tall woman should not think tall. The most famous fashion mannequins prove that you are mistaken in this view-point. These long-stemmed beauties stand around 5'8" and over, yet you'll never see them slouching their shoulders to shrink their size. The only actress I can think of who capitalized on poor posture was ZaSu Pitts.

KNOW YOUR TYPE

In dressing for success, figure analysis is of first importance, but knowing your type is almost as vital. Most successful stars have found their types, which if you think about it are very easy to spot.

Liz Taylor is the 'siren' type; Natalie Wood is the 'provocative' type; Sophia Loren is the 'sophisticated' type; Shirley MacLaine is the 'gamine' type; Merle Oberon is the 'elegant' type; and Audrey Hepburn is the 'chic' type. Whichever type *you* are should be seriously considered whenever you buy clothes or accessories. If you type yourself as 'sophisticated,' it is obvious that you won't buy little short white gloves and flat-heel patent leather shoes to wear with your new tailored suit. Leave these for the 'ingenue' type. If you're the 'wholesome' type, you're likely to look all wrong in slinky black bias-cut dresses. Play up your freshness with crisp, cleancut fabrics and clear colors. If you favor the glamor girl look, forget about white boots and above-the-knee skirts in favor of clothes with dramatic, figure-defining lines.

The new 'individualistic' type who can change with every picture includes: Jane Fonda, Virna Lisi, Candace Bergen, Tuesday Weld, Julie Christie, Samantha Eggar, Ann-Margret, Catherine Spaak, Sandra Dee, Geraldine Chaplin, Claudia Cardinale, Yvette Mimieux, Nancy Sinatra and Ursula Andress.

In many ways it is easier for you to retain the type you cast yourself in than it is for a movie star. When I dressed Shirley MacLaine for *What a Way to Go*, she played a part that required her to change her type with each of the five husbands she married in the picture. If you saw the movie, you'll remember that Shirley started as a simple small-town girl in gingham and blue jeans and moved her way up the financial and social scale with each man she married. From the bottom of the ladder to the top, it took about $500,000 worth of gowns and three million dollars' worth of jewels to bring about the final metamorphosis. She ran the gamut here from utter innocence to the peak of sophisticated glamor—and what she wore, plus her excellent acting, created each transformation smoothly.

In dressing to type there is one danger spot to watch for—going too far with your true-to-type dressing. Always bear your type in mind, but don't go overboard. Too much of a good thing is what caricatures are made of, and the last thing you want is to wind up looking like a cartoon. *Overdone* 'little girls' look more like comic valentines than ingenues, and souped-up sirens are strictly for the joke books. Hold the reins on your desire to be a type and you'll never look either like a clotheshorse, a circus horse, or for that matter, any part of a horse.

Once you have gotten the message about your own figure from the analysis recommended in this chapter, you are faced with a decision.

You can accept yourself as you are or you can decide, obviously, to improve your proportions through diet, massage and exercise. If this is your decision, don't buy any new clothes until you've achieved your goal. There's no point buying things for your present figure if there's a better one in your future. If, however, you have the will power of Shelley Winters you might approach your goal with a special incentive. Miss Winters is inclined to put on weight between pictures and whenever she's faced with the need to lose ten or fifteen pounds she goes out and buys several outfits that are too small for her. With the desire to wear the new clothes as bait, she diets down to fit the clothes. A good idea only if you have a whim of iron.

Whether or not you can do anything about improving your proportions actually, the right clothes can improve them visually. Try to think of this experiment in analysis as scientific. While you've only spent $4.95 on this book, the diagnosis it has enabled you to make is worth many thousands of dollars because it will help you to dress yourself more effectively for the rest of your life. The charts that follow this chapter are the prescriptions for your problem. Fill them. And refill them. They are sugar-coated in that their taste is good for *you*. But don't mix them up and take the pill intended for someone else.

FORMULA FOR ANALYZING YOUR FIGURE AND DRESSING TO IMPROVE IT

1. Analyze and get to know which basic figure type you are.

2. Do everything you can to improve what nature saw fit to give you.

3. Compare your size and type to the clothes chart for your best basic silhouettes.

4. Write down your assets and liabilities, and keep your measurements and analysis up to date.

5. Dress for success by wearing clothes that have been proven best for your type.

7

How to
USE COLOR
SUCCESSFULLY

7. How to Use Color Successfully

Color is probably more important than any other factor in dressing for success. It should be used like a precision tool to create a more pleasing image, and to make the most of what the good Lord gave you to work with in the first place.

In its first color movie, Hollywood reflected the accepted color ranges in women's clothing which were relatively basic and largely seasonal. There was the black cloth coat for winter, the navy blue for spring. White was for summertime and pastels were for evening. Bright vivid colors were confined almost entirely to accessories, and if they were worn in full costumes their wearer was considered 'fast.' From the beginning of time color has been a stimulator of both desire and appetite, and it has come to symbolize many things in many forms. The loveliness of a rose, the wickedness of a witch, the purity of the bride, the evil of envy, the luxury of royalty, the duplicity of the devil—all these bring vivid pictures to our mind in full and definite color.

Would the rose be the world's favorite flower if God had made it black? Would Eve have been as tempted by the apple had it been white? Would people bask in the sunshine if its rays turned them green? And if oranges gave forth dark purple juices would they be the nation's favorite breakfast fruit? Nobody knows the answers to these questions, but we do know that colors have a definite effect on us, as well as on the birds and the bees. Without color to attract there'd be no eggs in the nests, no honey in the hives—and no lipstick on the collar of your best friend's husband.

Color in your wardrobe is more than something to please the eye and more than just a matter of personal preference. It is a kind of magic that can transform you from what you are to what you would like to be. It can make you seem slimmer or fatter, younger or older, audacious or timid, dull or exciting, wholesome or naughty. But most of all, and for our purposes here, it can make you look better or worse. The colors you select for your wardrobe are as important as the make-up you choose for your face. Think of them, please, cosmetically. Color can do a lot for you—for your skin, your hair, your eyes and your figure.

Your natural coloring is the clue to the colors you should wear, because it is your complexion tone that is most affected by the colors you co-ordinate with it. If you have a naturally florid complexion inclined to high color and easy blushes, stay away from hot colors like rosy reds, oranges or hot pinks—and tone down your excited, over-the-washtub look by wearing cool beiges, pastels, gentle grays or navy.

Conversely, if your complexion is inclined to be ivory pale, zip it up with warm turquoise, lipstick pink and red or dramatize it with black, but stay away from all white if you don't want to look like the walking dead.

There are several groups of colors I want to discuss in this chapter, from the point of view of what they can achieve for you cosmetically.

The Elegant Colors: In the wardrobes of most well-dressed women you will notice a predominance of the marvelous neutrals. Colors that are quiet and unassuming in themselves but permit beauty of line and design to show through because they do not call attention to themselves. They are the quiet beiges, the heathery tones of gray, white, off-white, and of course, basic black. These are colors that are good fashion every year, and they know no season. They are fundamentals in the wardrobes of movie stars and women of fashion everywhere in the world. In the closet of the average woman who dresses on a budget, they present the advantage of economy because they form the background for endless versatility through the addition of different accessories. They lend themselves to the quick-change sorcery of bright scarfs, dramatic jewelry, colorful hats that keep them looking ever different, ever new.

The Young Colors: Young in spirit and in lively attention value, these colors are not necessarily confined to the young in years. Wear them if they compliment your complexion, to add a healthy glow to your skin, to brighten your eyes and to glorify the lights in your crowning glory. They are the sweet, innocent pastels—pink, blue, yellow—plus bright red and navy blue. I don't recommend a total bright red costume for anyone over twelve, but a touch of red on navy, white or black is often the next best thing to a face-lift. Fresh young pastels selected deftly for hats, scarfs, blouses and accessories can do a lot to put vitality into the look of a dark or neutral costume, and they are perfect youth-foils in spring and summer dresses, suits and sportswear.

The Slimming Colors: No expert is required, I'm sure, to tell you that a straight-cut black dress will take poundage off your figure faster than a week on hard-boiled eggs. Illusory, to be sure, but nevertheless satisfying is the chic little black dress that, perhaps for this very reason, has become the late-day uniform of smart women on every scene. However, if you tend toward the kind of full-blown beauty painted by Reubens rather than the fashionably stretched-out ladies of Modigliani, there's no reason why you should continually attire yourself in a completely black ensemble. There are other dark colors that are equally effective and which may be more becoming to your skin and coloring. Dark sable brown is a rich and wonderful color for slimming, and so is charcoal gray or navy blue, the latter having the additional attribute of being young, younger, youngest.

The Excitement Colors: These are the colors that never fail to get a second look. The vivids, the brights and the offbeat tones that tingle and seem to pierce the very atmosphere in which they appear. Very much in fashion favor in sportswear, many of them have been finding their ways into coats, suits and accessories to add sparkle, fun and amusement to the fashion scene. If one of them is right for you and has something to offer your own coloring in the form of flattery, by all means wear it. They include orange and capucine, peacock and Persian blue, emerald and chartreuse, purple, red and Schiaparelli's gift to fashion excitement—shocking pink.

Thirty years ago such colors were rarely seen outside a circus tent or a sultan's seraglio, but the trend toward more casual outdoor living—plus the breakdown in the conventionality of dressing—has split the color wheel into a brilliant kaleidoscope where everything goes *together*. Combinations that were once reserved for gypsy dancers and Italian block parties are now not only acceptable but downright chic. Persian blue with kelly green, purple with hot pink, chartreuse with aqua, orange with bright blue—are as fashion-right today in both costumes and home furnishings as Grandmother's passementerie trims were in hers. As far as a wardrobe filled with Excitement Colors is concerned, I feel it would be too frenetic for most females—to say nothing of their poor, long-suffering husbands. Like caviar and champagne—or more aptly like escargots and frogs' legs—these colors are marvelous in small doses, but as an everyday diet, no. Use them as conversation pieces, for at-home and sports clothes in small servings. If you wear them well make the most of hats, jewelry, scarfs and trims used as punctuation marks to more subtly colored costumes.

The Man-Pleasing Colors: There have been many things said and written about colors that attract the male animal. The controversy seems to be between red and blue. 'All men,' says one faction of the mystical, unnamed oracles who started this whole argument before any of us were born, 'love red. Why else would Adam have reached out so eagerly for the apple? Why do men always turn around to look at a woman in a red hat (particularly when she has a shape like Sophia Loren)? Why do men send red roses to express their devotion?' In this manner the 'Men Are Mad About Red' contingent beats the drums for its favorite color. The Blues counter this. 'Look what men buy for themselves. Blue. Blue suits, blue ties, blue-striped shirts, blue bathing suits. Count them. Men buy more blue than any other color,' they cry in indignation against the Reds. 'If a woman wants to please a man, she should wear blue.'

At the risk of being labeled a non-conformist, a renegade and an extremist on this never-solved issue, I stoutly state: 'Every man's *favorite* color is the color of a pretty girl.' Color her anything you wish, including sky-blue-pink. If on *her* it looks good, he'll buy it! For that reason I say the best colors for man-pleasing are the colors you look best in. And that brings us to the most important colors of all.

The You Colors: The *you* colors are, of course, the colors you look best in. Earlier, I urged you to analyze your figure. I ask you now to analyze your coloring. This is the only way you can possibly know which hues to hew to and what shades to shy from. On your way to the mirror pick up a pencil and pad. Right now. Bring this book with you. If the light over your mirror isn't good (why isn't it?) take a hand mirror to the window. Take a good honest look at your skin. Is it really fair? Is the pigment or coloring in your skin pinkish, yellowish, tannish? Are you dark complected, olive-skinned? Write your complexion tone next to 'skin' on the pad, qualifying it by one of the pigment adjectives mentioned above. Now what about your hair (whether natural or assisted by your beautician)? Write down next to 'hair' whether you are currently a blonde, brownette, brunette or redhead. Underneath that write 'eyes' and make a careful note of one of the following: Light blue, dark blue, hazel, gray, light brown, dark brown, green.

What you have written down is *you* in Technicolor. This is your Color Aura. What colors can be added to this picture of you to make you prettier, younger, more attractive, more desirable? Let's fill in the missing colors for your own portrait of success.

If you have a fair flawless skin the chances are all colors are reasonably becoming to you—but some will be more becoming than others. Blue-eyed blondes with such skin look marvelous in blues, particularly the soft aquas that make their eyes look like the Mediterranean. Redheads with the very same skin tone, but with gray eyes, should cultivate greens because of the chameleon-like changeability of their eyes.

ADVICE FOR SALLOW COMPLEXIONS

Regardless of the other colors in your 'picture' (eyes and hair) stay away from all colors that have yellow casts: Yellow, yellow-beige, orangey-red, yellow-browns, gold and tan. Light colors like pastels and white are good because they tend to make you look tan rather than yellowish. You can wear black, but it is best to have some lighter color, in the form of collar or trim, near the face. Rosy colors with a blue rather than yellow cast are good bets too. Here are some Color Aura recommendations for famous stars. Does your Color Aura match one of them?

Grace Kelly and Lana Turner: fair hair, fair skin, blue eyes.
    Best colors: All blues, greens, violet, purple and medium shades of brown. They avoid very light natural colors.

Julie Andrews: light brown hair, fair skin, blue eyes.
    Best colors: Blue, violets, soft gold, blue grays.

Nancy Kwan and France Nuyen: dark hair, golden skin, hazel eyes.
    Best colors: Reds and oranges in clear tones, ivory, pale pink, black
    and charcoal gray.

Sophia Loren: dark hair, olive skin, hazel eyes.
    Best colors: Pink, peach, apricot, beige tones, ivory and black, clear
    red and charcoal gray.

Elizabeth Taylor and Vivien Leigh: dark hair, fair skin, blue eyes.
    Best colors: Violet and purplish tones of blue among others. Warm
    peach-beige, pale pink, ivory.

Lena Horne and Eartha Kitt: dark hair, skin, eyes.
    Best colors: 'Grayed' tones of blue, green, pink-peachy-beige, ivory.

Natalie Wood: dark hair, fair skin, dark eyes.
    Best colors: Clear strong tones of red, blue, green. Warm apricot-
    beige, dark brown, ivory.

Samantha Eggar and Ann-Margret: red hair, fair skin, blue eyes.
    Best colors: Bright and medium greens, blue, violet, purple,
    medium shades of brown, beige, pastels.

Shirley MacLaine: brown hair, fair skin, blue eyes.
    Best colors: Apricot, mint green, pale pink, blue, pink-beige,
    medium shades of brown.

Barbara Stanwyck: silver hair, fair skin, blue eyes.
    Best colors: Gray, from light to charcoal, blue, violet, purple,
    bright to medium greens.

Kim Novak and Tuesday Weld: blond hair, fair skin, brown eyes.
    Best colors: Blues, violets, soft greens, golden beige, white.

Color is probably the most helpful and least costly element in dressing
successfully. Color can be your greatest friend or your worst enemy. It

can make you look younger or older, thinner or fatter, dowdy or smart.

I have worked out a complete Color Aura Chart with the correct colors to complement each other to help you in your own selection. I have not included black or white which to me are the most important colors in the entire range, because both black and white are a necessary part of every woman's color plan regardless of her color aura.

I have designed for practically every actress in the motion picture industry. Every one of them has her own Color Aura—and we use this chart as a basis for the color of her clothes.

THE PSYCHOLOGY OF COLOR

Actually most women, even stars, aren't conscious of this method. I know, because ever since I've been designing, one of the first requests an actress makes is, please don't make me wear red, or blue, or whatever color she dislikes. There is a deep psychological reason for this. She doesn't feel good in this color. People react differently to the same colors. Some women are depressed by green, distressed by purple or are suspicious about yellow. But overall, most women have definite feelings about the colors best for them.

Once I was designing a dress for Barbara Stanwyck to match a mink coat. This was before fur mutations and a mink was a mink-brown. Barbara took one look at the dress and said, 'Oh, no, not *brown*—I'd hate myself! I'd rather give up the mink coat.' If I had known then what I do now about Color Auras, I'd never even have thought of a brown dress for her. She doesn't feel good in brown and no one should wear a color in which she feels unlovely.

Kim Novak adores any shade of lavender or purple. Lee Remick, who is also a blonde, says, '*Anything* but lavender. I'd feel sick and probably would look sick.' Debbie Reynolds, who loves all shades of green, says they do something for her. Sophia Loren, with her own dramatic coloring, would just as soon wear nothing but black or white. Shirley MacLaine varies her Color Aura according to her role in a picture, but when she is her natural self (she is a brunette with very fair skin) blue makes her feel and look best. Natalie Wood feels and looks best in high-key clear colors—brilliant yellow, vivid scarlet and also black and white. Elizabeth Taylor's favorites are French blue, lavender and white.

Be sure of one thing: color can completely change not only the appearance, but the mood of any woman, whether she is actress or housewife.

Remember that in the world of fashion every season sees a new color emerge as *the* fashion color. It may be olive green, cinnamon brown, magenta, or peacock blue. But *don't* buy or wear any article of clothing in a color that is bad for you, no matter what the fashion oracles say. It's a great temptation when the saleslady says, 'But, Madame, this is the very *latest* color from Paris.' Be firm—remember that if your Color Aura is unfriendly toward that color, you will never look right or feel happy in it.

COLOR IS NOT HAPHAZARD

I firmly believe that color should be selected deliberately and for a reason, just as you would select food for different meals. You don't serve the same menu for a social luncheon as you do for a Boy Scout picnic—and you don't wear the same colors for every occasion. Color attracts the eye more quickly than any style or silhouette. Bold violent colors are out of place at places of worship or any occasion of solemnity—such as funerals or formal weddings. Somber colors should not be worn on occasions that call for festivity and fun.

Color is one of the greatest camouflages artists ever conceived, as the protective coloring of nature proves so well. I'm giving you all those camouflage rules in a subsequent chapter on successful fashion camouflage.

THE THREE BASICS OF YOUR COLOR AURA

Going back to the three basic parts of a Color Aura, let's accept the color of your eyes as they are. The color of your skin can be drastically altered, although I advocate very little major change. If an olive-skinned person has a great deal of yellow pigment, perhaps a warmer tone of make-up would be more becoming. If the complexion is dull and colorless, by all means use color to help.

In the field of make-up, I'm very definite about one rule: make-up should not look like make-up—it should not show. It should only accentuate your best points and help correct your defects. Nearly every magazine has charts on how to use make-up, and my rule is, if you don't know, find out. Go to a beauty shop or to the cosmetics departments of stores. Every line of cosmetics has charts and information on what to use and how to use it. Remember that color in make-up can be treacherous—especially for the senior citizen, because too much color only makes an older woman look older.

The third factor in your Color Aura is hair—and over that you *do* have complete control. Changing the color of your hair, which used to be considered 'fast' is now no more unusual than changing the color of your nail polish. But it also can be treacherous, because the color of your hair is part of your Color Aura and *must* not fight with the other two parts—the color of your eyes and your skin.

I believe that hair coloring is most successful when it brightens and intensifies your own natural hair color. However, this is an age of experimentation, and my advice is that if you are considering drastically changing the color of your hair, *try on a wig first*. Perhaps a new color may be becoming—do wonders for you, but it could be a disaster. At least, you can take the wig off!

On the subject of gray or white hair, I think they are beautiful. However, if there is any valid reason for a change—*change!* We in America are so impressed by the youth image that looking young is almost a mania. If gray hair gives you a feeling of premature age or if you feel it's a detriment in business, then cover the gray.

Some of the most beautiful women I know have silvery hair—Barbara Stanwyck for one—and I know gray and white hair is much softer and kinder to an elderly face than a brighter shade. However, this is a very personal subject, one that only you can decide. But if you decide to cover the gray, I suggest that you try to return to your original hair coloring rather than make an extreme change. And don't forget, every time you change the color of your hair, you change your Color Aura.

I have very definite views on color because I *know* what it can achieve—both for good and bad. Every time we start an important picture, we make screen tests of the stars in different make-up, hair colors and clothes. We don't guess—we find out. Sometimes we deliberately use a bad color to make a star look unattractive or old or vulgar or whatever we wish—because color, more than any other facet of fashion, can change the way you look.

Actresses have to know color. The way they look and dress is part of their careers, their lives, and many of the outstanding stars have very distinctive and unusual Color Auras. Take, for example, Lena Horne, one of the most glamorous women in the theatrical world. She has learned to dramatize her vivid dark beauty by wearing coral, pale aqua blue and white to emphasize her Color Aura.

A complete contrast is Carroll Baker—with very fair skin, very blue eyes and almost platinum-blond hair. She follows her Color Aura very closely by wearing platinum beige, flesh pink, and white.

The third, completely different, color type is that of Nancy Kwan with her golden olive skin and dark hair and eyes—and the colors that she wears are gold, scarlet, beige and olive green.

These are three distinct and different types of beautiful women with completely different Color Auras who have learned how to emphasize them by making color a further extension of their personalities.

Each Color Aura attracts other colors that are complementary—and the color chart will help you to pick out your most becoming colors. Remember, however, that no rule can be followed too dogmatically. If your Color Aura recommends the cool range for you, that doesn't mean you must dress entirely in those colors. A contrast is stimulating, and without it fashion could become monotonous. Don't be afraid of color, *experiment*. Try color accents—and don't forget that color is the greatest wardrobe-stretcher in the world. One dress or one suit can be radically changed by the use of color in jewelry, blouses and scarfs. For example, a beige or gray suit could be worn throughout the entire year by adding seasonal color accents: white for summer, russet for fall, bright scarlet for winter, and a pastel—pale pink, blue or yellow—for spring.

A woman can wear a neutral dress or good old basic black, and with the addition of different-colored hats and other accessories, present a completely different costume look.

Remember, bright colors attract the eye—don't use them in overdoses. A vivid color is best used in *small* areas such as accessories—and then not repeated too often. I much prefer to use a color accent only twice—for example, a black dress with pink hat and gloves, but never with the addition of a pink purse and pink shoes. In motion pictures we call these 'eye catchers,' and if the eye has to jump to too many areas, the result is confusing—and not good fashion.

Most of a woman's clothing budget goes into basic items—suits, dresses, coats, sportswear. In these basics you should use your own complementary colors—then use color accents to vary them and increase their use.

When you have studied your aura in the charts at the end of this chapter, you will see the basic complementary colors which should become the basis of *your* color selection. Now that you know your Color Aura—color yourself *beautiful!*

FORMULA FOR USING COLOR SUCCESSFULLY

1. Select your Color Aura from the chart.

2. Match it up with the basic colors recommended for your Aura.

3. Wear colors from those recommended that make you feel good. *Feeling good is looking good.*

4. Use color cosmetically *to make you look prettier, younger, taller, slimmer.*

The darker the color, the slimmer the figure looks. If you are heavy *all over*, wear medium dark to dark colors. This doesn't mean you have to wear black or somber shades, but be sure the *value* is dark! If you are heavy in certain sections, concentrate the dark colors in that area. For example: if your figure is small above the waist and heavy below—wear lighter colored tops and darker colors below the waist. And vice versa for the opposite figure type. Remember, light colors add weight, dark colors minimize weight.

TOO THIN?

Color can make you look heavier. The lighter the color, the heavier you will look. If you are *thin* all over, wear medium-light to light colors to give the illusion of more weight. If you are too thin in certain *areas*, concentrate on the use of light color on those areas and use the darker shades on the areas of the figure where you are heavier. For example: if you are top heavy—that is, heavy above the waist and too thin below— wear the darker colors above and the lighter shades below the waist.

TOO TALL? Color Can Minimize Height!

Use the 'color break' system. Wear a different color or color value top and bottom—skirt and blouse, skirt and overblouse, skirt and jacket or two-color dress. The same applies to pants and tops. Make a color break at the waistline with a contrasting belt, sash, cummerbund or tie.

TOO SHORT?

Avoid color breaks—use one color. Wear the same color value in either one-piece or two-piece dresses and in pants and tops. *Avoid* contrasting colors or belts that are too wide. Accentuate unbroken lines and constant color.

COLOR Can Make You Look Younger!

Color *value* rather than color itself gives the impression of youth. For example, light blue is more youthful than dark blue. However, a woman who wishes to look younger must realize that too 'youthful' a color such as baby blue or baby pink can do just the opposite and call attention to her age. The best color formula to make a woman look younger is wearing *medium* color values in the costume and *light* color values at the neckline.

COLOR Can Give You a Look of Maturity!

Color *and* color value can both help give a look of maturity, particularly with the use of the darker color range and the use of muted or grayed colors in the lighter and medium ranges. Obviously, darker colors tend to make any woman look more mature, and the absence of bright colors will have the same effect. For example, a soft bright blue can give a youthful look; a soft gray blue can give a look of maturity.

COLOR Can Make You Look Smarter!

Since color is so very personal, any woman will look smarter in the colors that belong to *her*—the colors she selects from her own Color Aura (see Color Aura Chart). The accepted 'smart' color varies every year and every season, but the really chic woman wears the colors that are becoming to her and never lets color overpower her.

COLOR Can Make You Look Dowdy!

Careless use of color can make any woman look dowdy. This means mixtures of colors which are not harmonious and which give an unpleasant effect—such as too-violent colors which do not belong in your Color Aura. The other extreme is the use of drab, ugly and monotonous colors without color accent or relief.

COLOR AURA CHART
Your Color Aura—and Your Colors!

Hair	*Skin*	*Eyes*	*Colors*
Black	Dark olive to dark golden olive	Dark brown to black	Coral, scarlet, beige, olive green
Black	Medium	Medium green, gray, hazel	Flame red, leaf green, jonquil, yellow, wood brown
Black	Fair	Light blue, violet	Violet, geranium red, rose pink, dusty blue
Dark brown	Dark olive to dark	Dark brown to black	Burnt orange, pastel yellow, cocoa brown, gold
Dark brown	Medium	Medium green, gray hazel	Pale rose-pink, blue violet, moss green, sable brown
Dark brown	Fair	Light blue, violet	French blue, crimson, mauve, deep violet

Hair	Skin	Eyes	Colors
Medium brown	Olive	Dark brown to black	Chrome yellow, jade green, light henna, camel
Medium brown	Medium	Medium green, gray hazel	Chartreuse, forest green, topaz, deep brown
Medium brown	Fair	Light blue, violet	Lavender, powder blue, spice pink, sapphire blue
Light brown	Olive	Dark brown, black	Fern green, fawn beige, blue gray, vermillion
Light brown	Medium	Medium green, gray, hazel	Rose beige, old gold, gray green, cinnamon
Light brown	Fair	Light blue, violet	Cherry red, blue violet, spruce green, gray
Dark red	Olive	Dark brown, black	Flame red, cocoa brown, beige, jade green
Dark red	Medium	Medium gray, green, hazel	Amber, brick red, lime green, forest green
Dark red	Fair	Light blue, violet	Blue green, shell pink, ivory, deep blue
Medium red	Olive	Dark brown, black	Coral, topaz, sea green, tobacco brown
Medium red	Medium	Medium gray, green, hazel pink	Antique gold, citron green, russet brown, melon

Hair	Skin	Eyes	Colors
Medium red	Fair	Light blue, violet	Aqua, strawberry pink, mint green, deep blue violet
Light red	Olive	Dark brown, black	Chartreuse, henna, apricot, mint brown
Light red	Medium	Medium gray, green, hazel	Moss green, peach, rust, gold
Light red	Fair	Light blue, violet	Pale turquoise, cinnamon, light blue violet, warm beige
Dark blond	Olive	Dark brown, black	Lacquer red, misty pink, nutria brown, citron green
Dark blond	Medium	Medium gray, green, hazel	Emerald green, mustard, bittersweet orange, light taupe
Dark blond	Fair	Light blue, violet	Shell pink, aqua, lemon yellow, bright navy
Medium blond	Olive	Dark brown, black	Beige, mocha brown, Chinese red, pine green
Medium blond	Medium	Medium gray, green, hazel	Tangerine, canary yellow, dark olive green, autumn brown
Medium blond	Fair	Light blue, violet, cranberry red	Peony pink, champagne beige, deep blue violet,

Hair	Skin	Eyes	Colors
Light blond	Olive	Dark brown, black	Brilliant orange, soft avocado green, deep pink, gold beige
Light blond	Medium	Medium gray, green, hazel	Ultramarine blue, mimosa yellow, strawberry pink, beaver brown
Light blond	Fair	Light blue, violet	Platinum beige, flesh pink, lavender, dark blue
Dark gray	Olive	Dark brown, black	Medium rose, claret red, amethyst, teal blue
Medium gray or silver	Medium	Medium gray, green, hazel	Pale turquoise, pale yellow, emerald green, raspberry red
Medium gray or silver	Medium	Light blue, violet	Silver gray, soft blue, ruby red
White	Fair	Light blue, violet	Violet, aqua, soft rose, sapphire blue

*

8

Success in Fashion
CAMOUFLAGE

8. Success in Fashion Camouflage

The recent popularity of Op art has made all of us aware of how easily the eye can be fooled with pattern and color. Camouflage, just as it deceives the enemy in wartime, can be utilized by you to help conceal your secret shortcomings. If you have seen any of the Op art exhibitions throughout the country you no doubt found it hard to believe that some of the paintings were standing still. Some looked as though they were whirling, others as though they were curved, wavy, concave or convex, and still others seemed to blink like Christmas tree lights. Op art, in dressing for success, is not new. Optical illusions are created everyday by women who choose fabrics and patterns for their clothes that achieve innocent deceptions. Dissatisfied creatures that they are, women are always wanting something they don't have. If they're tall, they long to be petite, and vice versa. If they're heavy, they want to be slim. If they're slim they want to be still slimmer. And sad to say, far too many of them go about achieving their goals in the wrong ways.

Take, for example, the tiny woman around five feet tall. You've all known one of these adorable little creatures who in her desire to 'grow' wears high spike heels and very tall hats. She winds up looking like a midget in somebody else's clothes. If, instead of her tall hat and stilt-like heels, she selected fabrics that elongated her body line, her goal would be achieved pleasantly and successfully.

For instance, tweeds and woven fabrics, with diagonal or spiral patterns lengthen the body, horizontal patterns shorten it. It is obvious also that a tiny woman should not wear bold patterns like oversized checks, stripes or polka dots. Small dainty patterns are far more in keeping with her size. Like her smaller body, head, feet and hands— her accessories should be scaled down. An oversized handbag on the arm of a very small woman always looks to me as though the bag is carrying her.

Another case is the very tall woman who tries to minimize her height by wearing flat-heel shoes and flat hats, and who walks round-shouldered. She also exaggerates the very characteristics she hopes to disguise. Her greater height calls for a hat proportioned to her size. It should be a large hat rather than a small one, because a large hat will make her look smaller. She can afford to wear bold patterned tweeds, large floral prints and bulky nubby woolens because she can carry the 'weight' of such patterns without looking overdone. She should cultivate heavy rather than dainty jewelry, medium-heel shoes rather than flats, two-piece costumes rather than shifts. These things will not only minimize her height, but make her look graceful and willowy rather than awkward.

As for the woman who desires to look thinner (is there any other kind?), most clothing designed today has slenderness as its goal. Certainly no designer creates clothes expressly to make women look heavier. The ruffles, bustles, frills and laces that once marked the 'fine figure of a woman' are gone forever, and in their place is the pared-down, simplified body-line dress that contrives to conceal curves rather than create them.

There are some rules, however, that you can follow if you are heavier than you should be or want to be.

Shun bulky, nubby and hairy fabrics in favor of sleek ones. Stay away from shiny surfaces like satin, sequins or lamé—they only spotlight and highlight extra pounds. Wear solid colors, preferably dark ones. Avoid short jackets and circular treatments that go round and round, such as peplums, contrasting belts, horizontal stripings. They make *you* look round. Keep your costumes all of a color, rather than contrasting skirts

to tops. Confine brilliant colors (reds, hot pinks, orange and so on) to small touches or trims. Wear clothes that fit *easily* rather than tightly. Clothes that fit like sausage skins make you look even porkier. Eliminate large-patterned prints from your wardrobe. Cultivate vertical trims (bindings, seamings, edgings, buttons and such) that go north and south rather than east and west. Stay on your diet.

While effective camouflage can do a great deal toward making you look more attractive and closer to your ideal, it is of first importance that

you accept the things about yourself that can't be changed. If you are too tall (according to *your* standards), think like a model. Hold yourself gracefully with your head high and your shoulders back. Remember that the great Ziegfeld searched the world over for beauties who towered six feet and over, and the famous fashion models who wear clothes so magnificently are all at least 5'8".

If you are shorter than average, think of the advantages of the 'little woman.' Men love the doll-like quality of tiny women who make the

---

most of their petite stature and their small feet and hands by wearing clothes that show them off. Think of the many diminutive movie stars and notice how they dress. Whatever your shortcomings are—whether you're too short, too tall, too chunky or too skinny—your clothes can perform minor miracles in concealing, camouflaging and disguising them. But your *attitude* performs the major miracles. Some very homely women with mediocre figures manage to look strikingly handsome because they 'Think Beautiful.' They enter a room as though they have all the attributes of a great beauty. They have self-confidence. Conversely, you surely have met women who have good features and figures who manage to *look* like frumps because they fail to capitalize on their assets.

FORMULA FOR THE SUCCESSFUL USE OF CAMOUFLAGE

1. Use color and design to improve your figure.

2. Accept the things you cannot change. Your liabilities may be turned into assets.

3. Develop confidence in your appearance and dress to match that confidence.

4. 'Think Beautiful.'

9

The
'SUCCESSORIES'
of Your Wardrobe
or Accessories Season the Costume

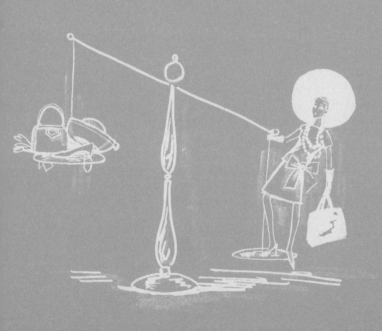

9. The 'Successories' of Your Wardrobe or Accessories Season the Costume

Accessories, those small wonders that can make such a big difference in the total effect of any costume, are as important as the coats, suits, dresses and sportswear you choose as the backbone of your wardrobe. They are not only the finishing touches that give you the look of perfection every woman desires, but they are also the magic touches that can turn one dress or suit into many. In a room full of women in 'little black dresses,' for instance, there is frequently one woman who stands out because of what she has added to that dress, so similar in style to all the others, that gives her costume distinction and flair. It might be a simply wonderful, flattering hat that makes her look prettier than all the others. It might be a dramatic necklace, an unusually striking pin or elegantly coordinated shoes and hosiery.

On the other hand we have all been jarred by the woman who has utterly ruined the effect of her little black dress by the blatant *overuse* of accessories. She stands out too, but the fact that she has strung herself with too many baubles, carried a handbag too big or used too much of one color in trying to co-ordinate shoes with her gloves *and* her hat, has turned her into a fashion caricature.

Accessories might well be thought of as the 'seasoning of your costume,' and as every good cook knows, while seasoning is the secret of culinary success, too much salt or an overdose of pepper can ruin the sauce. The same principle holds for the use of accessories, so take some advice from superbly dressed Claudette Colbert when she says, 'After I'm completely dressed I always take one long look in a full-length mirror, and if there is a single sour note in my ensemble, I eliminate it.' There has been a great tendency in the last few years, however, for women to go too far in their elimination of the 'successories' that add up to the perfect look. Even in our large metropolitan cities the trend to go hatless, gloveless and stockingless has grown by leaps and bounds. To me this *carefree* look, which should be confined to the very young, turns into a *careless* look when it is indulged in by mature women. I urge you, if you are over twenty-five, to consider the advantages of the costume-makers—the accessories.

HATS ARE FLATTERERS

Hatlessness is all right in certain places, but there is no flatterer (with the possible exception of a Latin lover) more certain to make a woman look younger and prettier than a becoming hat. We know one woman, very successful in the fashion world, who relies almost entirely on hats for her reputation as a fashion plate. Her claim is that if her hat is dramatic enough no one notices the rest of her costume, so she keeps her wardrobe of dresses and suits to a minimum—varying the look of each with a collection of wonderful hats. Hats, in addition, do wonders in covering up hair that needs 'doing.' They perform miracles in making an older woman look younger, a heavy woman seem slimmer or a plain woman more exciting. If you wear hats well, don't let the fad for hatlessness inhibit you. Wear them as you wear cosmetics, not as something to cover your head, but as something that makes you look prettier, younger and more distinctive. And choose them with flattery in mind.

ALL IS NOT GOLD THAT GLITTERS

Your jewel box may not contain a single emerald and be completely devoid of priceless heirlooms, but diamonds notwithstanding, I say, 'Jewelry is a costume's best friend.' Whether it's the real thing or what is called 'costume' jewelry, it should be chosen with the utmost care and worn sparingly except on the most formal occasions where the 'glitter-bugs' flash and shine in competition.

When you buy costume jewelry think of the purchase you are about to make this way: 'Would I buy this piece if it were *real* and I could afford it?' If the answer is no, don't buy it. It will be worn only briefly and then wind up in that junk pile of tarnished chains, links and single earrings every woman collects over a period of time. Rather than spend money on an array of gadgety trinkets, seek out jewelry pieces (real or costume) that will truly enhance your wardrobe. And consider your own physical deficiencies when you choose jewelry. If your hands are not as lovely as they might be, don't load them with big rings that call attention to them. If your wrists are pudgy, stay away from wide clunky bracelets. If your ears are too big for your head or stand out, don't try to minimize them with oversized earrings. Develop a jewelry style that is right for you. If you have wonderful blue eyes, wear turquoise. If you have red hair and green eyes, see what jade can do for you. Silver jewelry looks marvelous on silver-haired women, and while pearls look good on everybody, gold is particularly flattering to blondes.

GRACE NOTES

Handbags, gloves and shoes are the marks of elegance in any costume. They are the grace notes that pull an entire look together and they are also the sour notes that can kill the effect you want to achieve. The large tote handbag is a very fine thing when you consider all the necessities most women lug around with them, but it certainly becomes an eyesore when worn with a pretty afternoon dress or a soft dressmaker suit. Every woman needs at least three types of bags—the large spacious one for practical purposes (business, shopping, traveling), the ladylike leather bag to wear with suits and tailored dresses and the after-five bag of a luxurious material that can double in brass with both cocktail clothes and formal wear. For day wear it is a good idea to match your handbag to your shoes for a well-co-ordinated look. The exception to this rule is when you wear a bright colored shoe. Then, please, keep the handbag color subdued or neutral.

SCARFS AS COSTUME-CHANGERS

Pretty scarfs in an array of colors and patterns are among fashion's most versatile costume-changers. Not just tied around the head to keep hair neat on windy days, but used as collars or belts, for touches of color at a neckline or as tie-on tops with shorts. Scarfs are fun accessories that test your fashion ingenuity and imagination. Chiffon scarfs in pastel colors are really 'neck-romancers' when it comes to softening the throat-line of a simple dress. Gay printed scarfs add gaiety and spirit to the waistline of solid-color slacks and shorts. Adroitly draped and tied around a hat, a beautiful scarf can change an inexpensive hat into one that looks many times its cost.

One of the greatest mistakes women make in their use of some accessories is to use them as afterthoughts. They frequently plan their costumes carefully, including dress, hat and shoes—then simply throw on whatever jewelry first comes to hand and grab the handbag they wore yesterday. The result is a body blow to the total look. Another fashion *faux pas* involving accessories is failure to recognize the difference between the words 'access' and 'excess.' 'Access' opens the portals to where you want to go; 'excess' opens a Pandora's box of bad taste and ugliness.

Just as you analyzed the things in your closet (in Chapter 4), do an analysis of your accessories. Take all the gloves, handbags, shoes, jewelry, scarfs and hosiery out of their drawers and boxes and place them on the bed. Start sorting them out in co-ordinated groups. How many of your shoes have handbags to go with them? Do they go with the clothes in your closet in type (tailored, dressy, and so on) as well as color? Does your collection of jewels include the right types for your wardrobe, or is it all concentrated in one classification—too many earrings and no pins, too many rhinestones and no tailored gold pieces?

To make this chore more fun, pretend you're planning a fashion show. Take the clothes you wear most frequently out of the closet and start co-ordinating them into complete costumes with your available accessories. Do you find some costumes without a proper hat? Are there no shoes or handbags that belong with others? Would an attractive scarf add something to that dress? Write these 'missing links' down. First thing you know you'll have a real shopping list of things you need. On the other hand, if you find a pair of shoes, a handbag or jewelry that is left completely out because it doesn't go with *anything*, it's obvious you should *never* wear it—so get rid of it. When you have completed this experiment, you should have a number of well-co-ordinated outfits, and you will also know what to wear with what instead of haphazardly choosing your accessories on the run. If your accessories have been well chosen you will find they go with or complete *several* outfits, not just one. Few women have the money or the closet space to buy a complete set of accessories for every costume. This should be taken into consideration when you buy accessories, of course.

'What will it go with?' is the question to ask yourself whenever you try on a hat, select a handbag, purchase new shoes or fall in love with a

Don't let accessories "overbalance" you!

piece of jewelry. Naturally, your inventory of accessories should be kept firmly in mind when you buy clothes too. Is the suit or dress you're considering compatible with your on-hand accessories? Or does it call for the additional expense of a new blouse, hat, shoes, bag?

In a world where standardization of styles is very much with us, it is frequently the accessories a woman wears that give her a look of distinction. A season or so ago every other woman owned the Chanel-inspired suit with braid-trimmed cardigan jacket. Yet the variety of ways one woman accessorized it made it look entirely different from the similar suit her neighbor owned. Let accessories be your form of creative expression in building a wardrobe. When you tire of a dress or suit, consider before you discard it what you could put with it or add to it to make it look fresh and new. Experiment with changing the look of a costume and even its mood (from sportive to dressy, from casual to tailored) by the adroit use of accessories. You'll find your wardrobe will stretch and so will your budget. And at the same time, you'll put more fun into the art of dressing.

FORMULA FOR SUCCESSFUL ACCESSORIZING

1. Analyze the accessories you now own along with your clothing. Eliminate the unnecessary—fill in the missing links.

2. Wear accessories to 'spice up' your costumes—but don't overdo it.

3. Buy accessories that improve the Total Look you want to achieve.

4. Put your costumes together as though you were planning a fashion show.

5. Experiment with accessories to stretch your wardrobe.

10

The
'SECRETS OF SUCCESS'
or Underneath It All

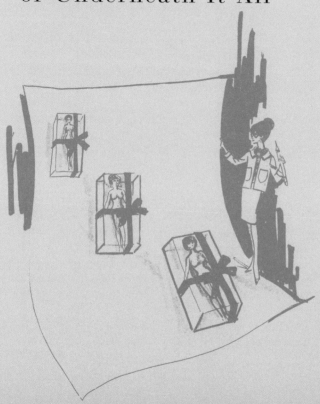

10. The 'Secrets of Success' or Underneath It All

A book about dressing for success without a chapter on fashion's vitally important 'undercover' agents would be as ineffectual as an Ian Fleming thriller without James Bond. Just as Bond is the one who holds things together and shapes up the ultimate triumph, so are your underthings the secret agents that shape *you* for success. The most lavish and beautiful wardrobe in the world won't get you the job, the man, the social position or whatever else you desire if what you wear underneath it all is out of date or out of shape.

Aside from the feminine delight and feeling of daintiness that pretty lingerie and foundations give you, today's designers have created garments for every purpose from lifting the bustline to rounding the bottom and from flattening the tummy to smoothing the thighs. What you can't do about your figure through starvation and exercise can certainly be improved through wearing the right foundation garment. There is no longer any excuse for a woman to be flat-chested or flat-bottomed. Bras and pantie-girdles fill in where nature failed. The waistline bulge is a thing of the past, if you will merely take the time to find a garment that eliminates it, and to have it properly fitted.

The time to buy new bras and foundations is when you buy new clothes. As fashion changes take place, the foundation people are 'with it,' and the contours of their garments are revised to do the most for your figure under the new clothes. The 'natural' look of recent vintage changed foundation garments from a rigid standard of control to a softly rounded line which looks better under shifts, knits and easy-fit garments. The younger, less aggressive bustline of recent years has been achieved successfully with bras that can be characterized as 'pointless.'

The pantie-girdle has come a long way from the brief thing it was a few years ago—developing a long-line of smoothness for the thighs, and for wear with jump suits, going all the way to the ankles.

The introduction of lightweight stretch materials has made it possible for any woman to be corseted (even the word seems obsolete) in complete comfort, while achieving the utmost in figure improvement.

The wildly popular pants craze which was started many years ago by Marlene Dietrich shows no signs of abating, but unless you look well in pants, or are willing to spend the time and money to equip yourself with a really efficient pantie-girdle, I say stick to skirts. And if you think your derrière looks all right without a girdle—in either pants or skirts—I suggest you get someone to take a moving picture of you from the back. Chances are you'll get the same reaction a cab driver did driving through Hollywood a few months ago. We were stopped for a traffic light when a plump ungirdled lady in a shift crossed the street. As he viewed her from the rear he shook his head and commented, 'It looks like there's two guys fightin' in there.'

When it comes to bosoms, the perfect feminine figure is a rarity. Yet ready-made clothing is made for perfect figures. No consideration is given to the proven fact that many women's bustlines are either too large or too small, too droopy, too flat and sometimes even lopsided. Knowing the score, top manufacturers of upper-story glamor have compensated for all these defects so that everyone can have a perfect bustline. And for those who want to have such a bustline twenty-four hours out of every day, there are even bras to sleep in.

Slips are also part of your secret for dressing successfully. Just because you have a lot of perfectly good slips from two years ago in your bureau drawer doesn't mean you should wear them. No matter how much you hike them up or adjust the straps, they're still too long and as the day wears on you'll be walking around with two skirts showing. As far as shoulder straps are concerned, the sleeveless dress has made it a must that you sew little ribbon 'anchors' in every dress so your slip and bra straps *never* show. There's nothing in the world that makes a woman look sloppier faster than a dangling shoulder strap, unless it's dirty fingernails. Get to the basic problem *before* buying clothes—start from the skin out.

Different clothes call for different foundations. If you think the very same undergarments will suffice for all the items in your wardrobe you're mistaken. While a lightweight all-in-one may be just fine under a loose-fitting shift, it is not adequate beneath the dress that is sheath-like in its line, requiring more control through the hips. There are long-line bras to eliminate diaphragm bumps. There are seamless girdles or tights to wear under knits and clingy clothes. You don't need all these in your wardrobe, but a successful outer wardrobe cannot be developed unless what goes underneath is considered. In many cases women leave clothes they never wear hanging in their closets just because they haven't got the right thing to wear under them. Every time they try those clothes on over that same old girdle they look the same—ungood. There's nothing wrong with the clothes themselves; there's something wrong with the shape underneath.

No one knows better than a studio designer how important underthings are in changing a woman's appearance. Take Julie Andrews for example: one type figure for *Mary Poppins*, another for *Torn Curtain* (a modern figure), another for *Hawaii* and a completely different silhouette for *Thoroughly Modern Millie*.

CHANGE THE FOUNDATION WITH THE SILHOUETTE

The time to buy new undergarments is not every time you buy something new, but every time there is a major change in the fashion silhouette—from loosely fitted to form-fitting, from long waistlines to short (or vice versa), from overblouses to high-busted Empire or from slim skirts to full. Each major change calls for something different, whether it be a bra, a girdle or an all-in-one.

Aside from the importance of your underthings in shaping your outer silhouette, there is the psychological factor of *feeling* lovely from the skin out. No matter how rich and elegant the clothes a woman wears on the outside, if her underwear and foundation garments are tacky, ill-fitting and mismatched she cannot feel right in her clothes. A surface beauty who is a mess underneath it all may fool her public, but the knowledge that she's wearing a blue bra, a white girdle and a faded pink petticoat pinned up at the hemline doesn't add to her self-assurance or self-esteem. A meticulous, fastidious movie star has put it, 'My mother always insisted we dress for an accident. By this she meant we should never be ashamed to have the doctor, nurse or anyone else see what we were wearing *underneath*.'

As far as love and marriage are concerned, the continuance of a perfect romance has often been halted in its tracks when a husband sees his bride in a lumpy old girdle and a sagging bra. By contrast, any woman can look fresh and attractive in a half-clothed state if her wardrobe of underclothing is as well co-ordinated, as well cared for and as well chosen as the costumes in her closet.

When you complete reading this chapter, I suggest you take a look at your undercover agents—the girdles, bras, slips and nightgowns in your bureau drawer. How many are out of shape? How many have stringy, stretched-out garters? How many are faded, tacky and unfit to be seen? How many can be co-ordinated into compatible 'sets' by color? If you wouldn't be caught dead in any of them, don't take the chance of wearing them while you're alive. They not only ruin the shape of your outer clothing, but they're poisoning your own mind about *you*. For a better dressed, more confident you, start at the bottom (of that bureau drawer) and build a new and better foundation for fashion with the right intimate apparel.

FORMULA FOR SUCCESSFUL DRESSING *UNDERNEATH*

1. Evaluate your present collection of girdles, bras, foundation garments for (a) condition, (b) efficiency.

2. Seek the advice of the experienced corsetière in your favorite store to find the right garment to improve your figure.

3. Buy underwear (slips, petticoats) that co-ordinates with your foundations in color, trim and type.

4. Remember that last year's shape may be wrong for this year's silhouette.

5. If you wouldn't want anyone to see you in your undies— get new ones.

11

How to
SHOP FOR SUCCESS

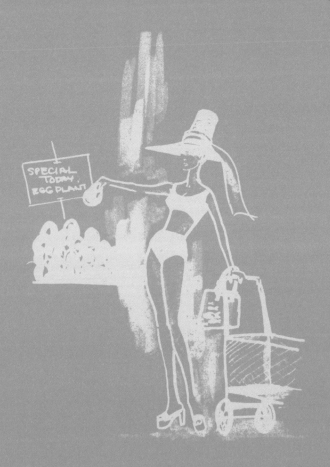

11. How to Shop for Success

The average female shopper can learn a lot about how to assemble a successful wardrobe by following some of the principles established in the business of retailing. In the store you shop in there is a buyer for each fashion department—dresses, coats and suits, sportswear, and so forth. When a buyer buys successfully her merchandise moves quickly off the racks. When she makes mistakes the merchandise is marked down for clearance. If she has too many markdowns over a period of time she is personally 'marked down' and cleared out of her job.

The same idea holds true in personal shopping. If you buy intelligently the merchandise *moves*—*out* of your closet and *out* of the house. It is worn and used frequently and enjoyed repeatedly. If it just hangs there, never seeing the light of day (or night), it is a liability and deserves to be 'marked down' by you. If you can sell it to someone else, clear it out. If you can't sell it, ditch it. A closet full of 'markdowns' is dangerous. You look at the amount of stuff on hand and find it hard to justify new purchases. Like a department-store buyer, you are overstocked with merchandise that won't move, and the older it gets the less it's worth to anybody.

SHOP WITH A PLAN

Some of the rules of successful store-buying can be easily used by you in assembling a successful wardrobe. First, like the buyer in a store, you should have a seasonal budget and shop with a definite plan. Your plan should be based on what your activities will be during that specific season, what new clothing you will need and how much you can afford to spend. If you set these important facts down on paper in an orderly fashion and then shop to the plan, you won't go over your budget or wind up with a lot of markdowns that never move out of *your* stock (closet).

Here's an idea of how such a completed plan might look for a spring season with a total clothing budget of $150.

Activities	Clothing on Hand and Still Good	Clothing Needed	Can Afford to Spend
Business	Blue wool dress	Soft dark suit	$60.
	Tweed suit	Blouse	$10.
Dates	White sequin sweater	Long skirt	$15.
	Black crepe dress	Cocktail dress	$40.
Sports	Gray pleated skirt	Sweater	$12.50
	Gold stretch slacks	Shirts (2)	$12.50
	Red sweater		

With such a plan you would go shopping with specific items in mind and get what you really need at the prices you can afford. In fact it is just like going food shopping with a planned menu. You wouldn't go marketing without a list of what you need to cook a meal, would you? Well, it's even less wise to shop for clothing without specifics in mind. If you make a plan—stick to it. Don't wander off into some kind of dream world (store advertising and fitting-room mirrors have this effect on some women) and buy things that have nothing to do with your plan, like the woman who desperately needed a new winter coat but instead spent her budget of $150 on a blond wig. She felt fine until the mercury dropped. When winter came and she had to wear her old moth-eaten out-of-date coat, she really flipped her wig.

After you make your basic plan, decide on the color of the clothes you plan to buy. Consider (a) your most becoming color, and (b) the most versatile colors to go with your existing accessories. Taking our hypothetical plan, for instance, it is important for our lady shopper, who owns a gray pleated skirt and a pair of gold slacks, to take both of them into consideration when she buys her new sweater and two shirts. The red sweater she owns will go with the gray skirt, but not with the gold slacks. Her choice of colors for the *new* sweater is limited to gray (matching the gray skirt and looking well with the slacks), gold (matching the slacks and going well with the skirt) or a complete contrast that will look well with *both* items—black, brown, hunter green, or peacock.

In choosing her new cocktail dress she must remember she already has a black crepe dress for dates. She should select a lively shade for her new going-out costume, such as a pastel that flatters her complexion. If she wants to get the utmost out of it she'll consider a jacket costume that can be worn with or without the jacket for different occasions, and which will last longer than the spring season because it will be adaptable to summer wear too.

The soft dark suit she chooses for business should be one that can be dressed up for after-five wear. It should not be too sporty in flavor because she already owns a tweed suit that can double for business and football games. If she selects the suit in a neutral tone, her sweaters and shirts (both old and new) will go with it, giving her additional changes. Her planned purchasing will not only help her make a limited budget go further, but it will help her develop a *co-ordinated* wardrobe.

Self-control is as much a factor in successful shopping as it is in successful dieting. If your diet calls for a thousand calories a day but you just can't say no to the desire for an added five hundred, you know you won't lose weight. If you want to keep your wardrobe lean and vital, don't get carried away by an irresistible bargain you don't need. Remember, you really can't *afford* a bargain unless it fits into your *plan*.

The traps women fall into when they shop *without* a plan are obvious. Not knowing what they need, they cannot know what they want—so they wind up buying more closet-fatteners.

Another good reason for planned shopping is the confusion created by the large selections of merchandise available in the average big store. It is extremely easy to be tempted by the innumerable goodies on display or be influenced by eager-to-make-a-sale store personnel who tell you you look 'simply divine' in everything.

Planned shopping is not only a boon to the budget-minded, but to the affluent woman too. Movie stars plan their wardrobes carefully for each season, and while their clothes collections are naturally more extensive than the average woman's, the best-dressed stars constantly weed their closets to keep their stock in prime condition. The woman who really plans her shopping to fit her needs always has the right thing to wear available. And she also has more money in the bank for extra needs that come up from time to time.

FORMULA FOR SUCCESSFUL SHOPPING

1. Think like a store buyer and analyze your stock.

2. Get rid of the 'fat' in your wardrobe.

3. Make a shopping plan based on what you have plus what you need.

4. Plan your wardrobe each season by color, by activities and by budgeting.

5. Stick to your plan.

12

BASIC WARDROBE
CHARTS

12. Basic Wardrobe Charts

A good basic wardrobe, like a good basic piece of furniture, sits squarely on four legs:

1. *Budget*
   How much money can you spend?

2. *Locale*
   Where do you live and work? In a city? Large or small? Suburbs? Country?

3. *Activity*
   What kind of life do you live? Social? Quiet? Busy? In business?

4. *Personality*
   Feminine? Sophisticated? Tailored?

A girl working in a large metropolitan city will need more sophisticated clothes, both for her work and social life, than one working in a small rural area. The same applies to the housewife. But basically every girl and woman has *two sets of clothes*—her 'uniform' or working clothes, whether she sits behind a desk or is keeping house for her family; and her 'off-duty' clothes for leisure, sports and social activities. Some of you may need more 'uniforms' than 'off-duty' clothes. *You should spend your money on the clothes you wear the most.* If you rarely wear a formal and need work clothes, concentrate on those. If your work demands very few changes of wardrobe and you lead an active social life, spend your money on the after-work wardrobe. Your clothes must suit the way you live and the kind of person you are! Clothes that hang in a closet most of the time are a bad investment. Buy clothes that work for you! And with you.

NOTE: When the number of articles is indicated, it means the number of articles of clothing. They can be all one type or a mixture of the varied types suggested. For example: if the list includes one suit, one dress and one 2-piece costume, it means three changes of clothing. It can mean three suits, three dresses or three costumes—or any combination of the three.

BASIC WARDROBE FOR THE WORKING GIRL
(single or married)

Most of you have two wardrobes—one for warm and hot weather and one for cool and cold weather. This basic wardrobe chart applies to both. The principal seasonal differences will be in fabric and color.

MORNING (Before work—at breakfast, etc.):
2 shifts or smocks or dusters or zipper-front step-ins or breakfast coats or robes

AT WORK (When no specific costume is required):
2 suits
6 tops—blouses or shells or sweaters
2 day dresses (1-piece, or 2-piece or jumper-type) and a separate jacket or cardigan
2 skirts to be worn with the jacket or sweater and blouses from above
1 coat

NOTE: If you prefer suits to dresses or dresses to suits, wear the type most becoming. I prefer any version of the suit or 2-piece costume—skirt and top—as it is more convertible.

This list applies to a girl who works in a place of business where appearance is important, or in larger cities. In smaller businesses or towns, one suit and less tops would be sufficient, and perhaps more blouses, skirts and sweaters are what would be worn in that locality.

LUNCH TIME:
If you have a luncheon date, fresh gloves and jewelry or any accessory you can bring with you can be added to your basic costume for a lift. Many girls who like a change at noon carry a large handbag for this purpose.

AFTER-WORK DATE:
If you are going out after work and don't have time to go home and change, take some instant glamor with you to work: a little veil or bandeau for your hair, pretty jewelry, gloves or a chiffon scarf. Some girls who wear suits to work carry a 'dressup' shell for evening dates.

AFTER WORK (with time to go home for a change):
1 costume (1-piece or 2-piece dress) and a jacket or wrap
1 cocktail or short dinner dress (try to use the wrap from above)
1 dressmaker or cocktail suit, with three changes of tops (knit, lace, crepe, matching fabric or brocade)
1 coat (unless you can use the coat from the costume #1 above)

I prefer interchangeable clothes whenever possible, such as the 'costume look' of a skirt with several tops and a matching jacket or coat. This costume can also have a matching long skirt for more formal wear and can be varied by different tops. It is important to remember that many single girls in cities have a larger date wardrobe.

AT HOME (entertaining):
1 hostess gown or hostess pajamas
1 at-home skirt or pants, more if you're married—with extra

---

interchangeable tops.

3 tops for above—blouses or shells or pullover sweaters. (*Important note*: These can be the same tops you use with your date clothes.)

2 dresses—1-piece or 2-piece (for informal entertaining)

NOTE: Many girls today emphasize the use of pants or hostess pajamas for home entertaining. These are easy to interchange with different tops. They make the use of separates an indispensable part of the modern girl's wardrobe.

AT HOME (Not entertaining):

1 housecoat or slip-on

1 lounging pajamas and tops, or pants and tops

FORMAL WEAR:

1 informal or semi-formal costume

This can be a dress and wrap or a dress and coat. It can be the same dinner dress you use for entertaining at home. If this is a 2-piece dress, get alternate tops which are great wardrobe stretchers.

1 formal evening dress and wrap, if you have use for it. (If not, get two semi-formal costumes)

I like the idea of the 'convertible costume' which is sold in most stores—one long and one short skirt of the same fabric, to be used with the same top and wrap. Many evening costumes can be changed by adding an evening sweater or stole.

Remember, the formality of an evening dress depends much on the type worn in the community and by your friends. Many single girls who work find their social lives call for more cocktail or dinner dresses, or even afternoon dresses, instead of more formal wear. But nearly any dress, suit or costume can be varied and changed by accessories—a dinner hat, a hair ornament, pretty shoes, gloves and jewelry. What I have given you is only the *basic* formula. Sometimes you should spend extra money on an extra dress or blouse or jewelry. Your clothes should be selected to fit *your* way, *your* environment and *your* type. If you don't look well in cocktail suits, don't wear them—wear dresses or costumes. If you don't like long dresses, don't wear them. Remember, fashion today is very flexible, and you can select what is right for you and your kind of work and play.

BASIC WARDROBE FOR THE SUBURBAN HOUSEWIFE

MORNING (Getting the family to work and school):
5 morning outfits (shifts or wrap-arounds or smocks or pants and tops, zippered step-ins, or housedresses)

HOUSEWORK:
4 aprons to go over the above, or coveralls, jump suits or work clothes

SHOPPING (At the market or for the house):
3 simple, casual day dresses, or skirts and tops, or pants and tops, sweaters, or sports clothes

SHOPPING (In stores other than markets):
3 sport suits or sport dresses, or separates, sweaters and skirts

NOTE: In many suburbs women wear pants for all kinds of shopping. This depends upon the accepted look of the community, and above all, if they are *becoming to you.*

LUNCH (Casual, in suburbs):
Same wardrobe as used for store shopping.

LUNCH (Semi-formal or formal at restaurants, clubs or friends' homes):
1 afternoon dress (1-piece or 2-piece)
1 dressmaker suit
1 costume (dress plus a jacket, scarf or wrap)

NOTE: If you are a 'dress' girl, three dresses and a wrap instead of the suit.

LUNCH (At home with guests):
Informal:
3 dresses, or a skirt and top, or pants and top
Formal:
1 afternoon dress (1-piece or 2-piece), the same as for lunch at restaurants and clubs, or a short hostess skirt or hostess pants with tops (blouses, pull-ons or shells)

NOTE: In very warm weather, long summer hostess skirts or hostess dresses, printed or plain, are popular at lunch and tea time.

AFTER FIVE (Tea or cocktails at a restaurant, club, tearoom or friend's home, or dinner):
1 cocktail dress
1 cocktail suit (dressmaker suit)
1 costume (dress plus a jacket, coat or wrap)
(This adds up to three outfits, which can be combined and interchanged)

AFTER FIVE (At home for tea or cocktails with guests):
1 cocktail dress (from above) or a hostess skirt, or pants with three tops (shells, fancy sweaters or blouses)
2 casual sports outfits (silk or knit), or skirts and tops, or knit dresses

DINNER AT HOME (With family):
4 housedresses, skirts and tops, or pants and tops

DINNER AT HOME (With guests):
Informal:
2 day dresses, or skirts and tops, or pants and tops
Semi-formal or formal:
2 cocktail dresses, or at-home skirts and tops, hostess pajamas or
hostess gowns
More formal:
1 long or short dinner dress
1 hostess gown or hostess pajamas

PARTY CLOTHES (At home, country club, friends' homes,
restaurants or hotels):
2 short evening dresses plus a wrap, or costumes (dress plus matching
wrap)
1 long evening dress or costume (if necessary)

NOTE: I can't emphasize strongly enough the importance of separates for women with limited budgets—the combination of mixing
skirts, long and short, with different tops and wraps.

BASIC WARDROBE FOR THE CITY HOUSEWIFE

MORNING (Getting family ready for work and school):
4 wrap-arounds or smocks or brunch coats or zippered step-ins, shifts,
pants and tops or housedresses

HOUSEWORK:
4 aprons or work smocks or work coveralls

SHOPPING (In the neighborhood, market, etc.):
2 sport suits with three changes of tops (blouses, shells or sweaters), or
two skirts with jackets or cardigans to be worn with the tops above
2 simple day dresses (1-piece or 2-piece)
1 sport or day coat

NOTE: Many women wear pants for marketing, even in cities—very
few should.

SHOPPING (And other city day activities):
1 day suit with three different tops which can be tops from the sport suit above
1 day costume (dress plus coat or jacket), which can be the same as for marketing
2 day dresses (1-piece or 2-piece)
1 day coat, which can be the same as for marketing

   NOTE: There is very little difference in wardrobe for the different kinds of shopping, though marketing indicates a more casual look.

LUNCH IN THE CITY (Matinee, tea, museum or art gallery):
1 dressmaker suit or afternoon costume (dress with jacket or coat), or two of one kind
2 dresses (1-piece or 2-piece)
1 wrap (coat, jacket, stole, etc.)

LUNCH AT HOME (Tea or cocktails with guests):
2 afternoon dresses or at-home skirts or pajamas, plus tops, or a simple hostess gown

NOTE: I prefer the 2-piece combination of skirt or pants and tops, as they are more interchangeable. However, many older women prefer the conventional afternoon dress.

DINNER AT HOME (With family):
4 dresses (1-piece or 2-piece), shifts or dressmaker, or combinations of skirts, pants and tops

DINNER AT HOME (Informal, with guests):
1 afternoon dress or short dinner dress
1 hostess gown or hostess pajamas

NOTE: The use of pajamas depends entirely on personal taste. If you don't like them and *they are not becoming to you*, substitute a dinner skirt and top or another dress.

DINNER AT HOME (Formal):
1 long or short dinner dress

NOTE: Many hostesses wear formal hostess gowns.

DINNER (At a café or restaurant, or theater):
1 dinner or evening dress from above, plus a wrap
1 dinner or evening suit, or costume (dress plus jacket or wrap or coat).
A short skirt is preferable for this type of dress unless the theater is a
formal opening.

PARTY WEAR:
Clothes from above for informal party wear
2 short formals (with wrap—a jacket or coat) or costume (dress plus
matching wrap)
1 long formal and wrap (optional)

NOTE: The use of separates or mixers is excellent for the city housewife. The option of a long or short skirt to wear with one top or jacket
is a great wardrobe stretcher.

WRAPS—FURS

In the basic list, I use the word 'wraps' to mean coats, jackets and
stoles. This is a very important part of your wardrobe. There was a time
when if I had said a fur-trimmed jacket or coat, or a fur stole or scarf, it
would have been out of the reach of the average girl or woman with a
budget problem. Now there are so many fur-trimmed jackets and coats
made with inexpensive or synthetic furs and even fur scarfs, capes, jackets and coats, that for the cool seasons—fall, winter and early spring—a
fur or fur-trimmed wrap is not only functional but adds importance to
any costume. A great many women with budget problems, who cannot
afford seasonal wraps, have a detachable fur collar, cuffs or scarf which
can be taken off their wraps in warm weather.

ACCESSORIES

No one, not even a designer, can tell any woman exactly how many accessories she will need. However, basically, for each season I suggest the woman, whether a working girl or a housewife, have two pairs of day shoes, one pair of dress shoes, two day purses and one evening purse. And since I am a firm believer in hats, at least two day hats and one afternoon or dress-up hat.

Jewelry is very personal and I believe that it should be separated into two categories. For day I prefer plain jewelry rather than 'glitter.' Evening jewelry can be glitter or pearls.

Scarfs, I think, are very important because they can easily change the look of a suit or costume.

Your need for rainwear and umbrellas naturally depends upon your locale and how much you would use them. Incidentally, rainwear is so attractive nowadays that you don't have to look like an orphan of the storm just because the weather is bad.

What you wear underneath your outer clothes is again a personal choice. Your selection of bras, girdles, foundations of all sorts, slips, half-slips, stockings, nightwear, wraps and so on depends on where you live, and how much you can spend, as well as on the dictates of current fashion.

List your wardrobe —

Keep an inventory —

SPORTSWEAR

This applies to all four categories:
  Working Girl—Single
  Working Girl—Married
  City Housewife
  Suburban Housewife

ACTIVE SPORTS

If you participate in active sports, be sure to shop in a specialty shop or the department of a store where the correct clothes are sold for the specific sport, whether it's tennis, golf, swimming or skiing. Obviously you can pick the color most becoming to you, but don't experiment with inventing your own active sportswear—it should be completely functional and fit in with what is traditionally worn for sport.

The amount of active sportswear you need will depend on how much you plan to participate. Above all, be sure that your accessories are correct—tennis shoes for tennis clothes, golf shoes with golf wear, and so on.

SPECTATOR SPORTSWEAR

The basis for spectator sportswear is the use of *casual* clothes: sports dresses, sports suits, separates, sweaters and skirts, pants and tops, culottes, jackets and sports coats. This, again, depends on what sports you are watching, the locale and the weather.

The number of garments you need will depend on how often you will use these clothes. Spectator sportswear, however, has become part of the suburban or country look and is used extensively in smaller towns and suburbs for day wear.

FABRICS

Except in extremes of weather, the look of modern clothes doesn't vary greatly during the four seasons. It is the *fabric* which indicates time of year. In the preceding charts, for all clothing which requires care—house clothes, work clothes and hot weather clothes—the fabrics most used are the easy-to-take-care-of blends and synthetics. The new wonder fabrics of today are drip-dry and crease-resistant in all manner of materials which make modern living much easier for both the working girl and the housewife. Even in the warmer fabrics, there are many new miracle blends which resist wrinkles and are easy to keep pressed and cleaned.

In the warm-weather group are linen, cotton, denim, poplin, piqué, seersucker and all forms of synthetics. For cool or cold weather, the warmer fabrics are wool, corduroy, jersey—and again, all manner of blends and synthetics.

Fortunately, most manufacturers indicate on their labels the content of fabrics and how they should be taken care of. The same thing applies to fabric bought by the yard.

Many people write to ask me what constitutes a day dress, an afternoon dress or a dressy dress. Here is where *fabric* is important because the silhouettes of modern design do not differ greatly for different occasions. For example, the same dress for day wear could be of cotton, piqué, seersucker or a synthetic; for luncheon or afternoon wear, it could be made of silk linen; and for after-five and dressier wear, it could be transformed by the use of crepe, silk jersey or silk print. The same silhouette could also go into informal evening wear if it were made of lace, chiffon or a dressier fabric.

Career Chart in Sizes

A SIZE 6, 8, 10

SUITS:

JACKETS—bolero, waist length, hipbone length. Can be boxy, semi-fitted, fitted or belted. SKIRTS—slim, flared or pleated. SLEEVES—short, 3/4 or full length. NECKLINE—high or open. FABRIC—plain, textured or patterned. COLORS—light, medium, dark—but not too vivid.

DRESSES:

1- or 2-piece—if 1-piece, choice of high, natural or dropped waistline. BODICE easy or fitted. SKIRT slim, flared or pleated. COLLAR, CUFFS and POCKETS good details. BELTS important accessory for small waistlines. COLORS can be light, medium or dark but not too bright. FABRICS that do not stretch, cling or sag. Can be plain, small-patterned or textured.

SEPARATES:

Wonderful for 'stretching' wardrobe as they can be interchanged. Employers favor formula of SKIRT, BLOUSE or SWEATER plus JACKET. JUMPERS also good for younger wearers. Color and fabric selection same as for dresses.

B SIZE 12, 14, 16

SUITS:

JACKETS—hipbone length or longer. Boxy or semifitted. SLEEVES—
3/4 or long. NECKLINE—medium or deep opening. SKIRTS—easy,
flared or pleated. FABRIC—plain, textured or small-patterned.
COLORS—medium to dark, neutral colors.

DRESSES:

2-piece dress excellent. With 1-piece dress, normal waistline preferable.
Normal belts; slightly bloused bodice. SKIRTS—easy, pleated or flared.
Collar and cuffs good detail for business dresses. FABRICS that keep
shape and fit loosely, plain or textured, or very small pattern.
COLORS—medium, medium dark to dark.

SEPARATES:

Use skirts with ease or action pleat; blouses or pull-ons with jacket or
cardigans. Color and fabric selection same as dresses, except if hips are
large, use darker color in skirt. If above waist is large, use darker color in
that area.

C *SIZE 18, 20 & UP*

SUITS:

JACKETS—hip length to $3/4$ length—straight or boxy. SLEEVES—$7/8$ to long. NECKLINE—narrow vertical opening—collars and reveres good detail. Keep ALL detail vertical. SKIRTS—easy, flared or use action pleats. FABRIC—plain or textured—no shiny surfaces. COLORS—medium dark to dark.

DRESSES:

1-piece-dress preferably. BLOUSED BODICE—narrow, non-contrasting belt. NECKLINE—V—with or without collar. SLEEVES—$3/4$, $7/8$ or long. SKIRTS— soft or with action pleats. FABRIC—dull finish or very small texture. COLORS—medium dark to dark.

SEPARATES:

For this size range do not break body line with contrasting colors or fabric. Instead, use one-piece dress or skirt and top of same color. Then add jacket or cardigan in same color range.

13

Nothing Succeeds
LIKE SUCCESS

13. Nothing Succeeds Like Success

Ever since man dragged himself out of the primordial slime and began to walk upright, clothing has been of vital importance. Originally it was merely an essential of survival. Without animal hides and furs the Eskimos would have frozen themselves out of existence. Without straw and feathers the equatorial savages would have been burnt to a crisp by sun and heat.

In the beginning clothing was worn for protection from the elements and the rough undergrowth of bush and jungle. But as man's sensitivities to beauty developed, even clothing designed for protection took on aesthetic qualities. The tough iron mail of the early crusaders was elaborately chased and ornately decorated to make a knight in shining armor a vision of amour. Clothing soon became a symbol of wealth and position, and while the lords and ladies of the royal courts dressed in rich and fashionable clothes, the serfs were clad in rags.

Today fashionable clothing is for everyone, in every income bracket, because it is as possible to be well dressed on a limited budget as it is on a vast income. What you wear is up to you. Once you dress yourself for success—whether your success goal is in business, love, matrimony or your rightful place in society—you have already taken the first step up the ladder.

Throughout this book I have tried to give you analyses to make, rules to be followed and formulae to guide you. Some of the world's most glamorous movie stars have used these ideas to make themselves more attractive to others. A basic premise followed in Hollywood is: 'If it isn't pretty, make it pretty.' And at the risk of repetition, I assure you that even the most beautiful women are not pretty all over. They have merely learned to use clothes deftly enough to give others the impression that they are. Why shouldn't you?

Perhaps some of the chapters in this book have not applied directly to you, while others have. I suggest that you go back and read over the chapters that can help you the most in achieving the success you want. And don't think that just reading and understanding a few thousand words will make an overnight difference in your life. You will still make some mistakes, because you are human. In spite of all I have said about how you should dress, you will still follow some of the dictates of your heart rather than Edith Head, and you will occasionally buy the wrong dress or suit or shoes or handbag. You may sometimes get carried away and purchase things you don't need and may never ever wear. Once in a while you might forget that your hips are wide, your neck is short, your shoulders round or your arms flabby and wind up with an unbecoming skirt or neckline or sleeve. It is not only human to make mistakes, it is feminine. (Think of all the women who have married the wrong man!) If you follow the ideas in this book, however, I can guarantee that you will understand yourself better and you will make far fewer mistakes in dressing for success.

I am convinced that if you constantly bear in mind all the major dangers to your success which lurk on every clothes rack and in every showcase in every store across the land, you, like the connoisseur of fine wine, will learn to distinguish between what is second-rate and what is great—for *you*. Once you have achieved this skill—the skill of knowing the silhouettes, the colors, the necklines, the sleeves and the skirts that are bad for you—you will eliminate them as fast as a good film editor removes unnecessary footage from a movie. You will also find it easier, faster and more fun to shop for clothes without the indecision and lack of confidence that plague many women. You will no longer find it necessary to bring your best friend along to ask her what *she* thinks when you try on a dress or coat or hat. You'll know what's right the minute you look at it and won't run the risk of having her tell you you look great in something that makes you look fatter, older and less attractive than she.

Just as a palate for certain foods (like olives, caviar or anchovies) has to be developed, your taste for the right clothes must be developed. If you follow the rules you will steadily educate your fashion palate to hunger only for the clothes that do something for you and that help you on the road to success.

In this last chapter we want you to consider another very important factor in your success. What you have on your back is one thing—but *what have you got on your mind?*

As you dress your body for success, your mind must also be properly arrayed for it. All the glad rags in the world won't bring you success if your mind is nothing but a grab bag of raggle-taggle odds and ends or non-descript patches and pieces. Just as I advised you to get your wardrobe in order, I insist you organize your mind.

Some women *think* they want success, but they suffer from naked minds—with nothing on them. Others *say* they want success but dress their minds in the gloom of defeat. Still others *pretend* they want success but let their minds tell them, 'Everything I *really* want is impossible.'

Dressing your mind for success is the first step toward achieving your goal. Dress it with decision, not confusion. There must be something you want more than anything else. Is it something that is possible for you to get? If not, get it *off* your mind and start again. What is the *next* thing you want more than anything else? Ah! Now we're getting some-place. If you can achieve *this* goal, it's better than not achieving the other, isn't it?

If you lack the looks or figure to become a Hollywood star, maybe you've got what it takes to be the best hostess in town. If you missed out on the ancestral wherewithal to make you an heiress, perhaps you have the brains and energy to make your daughter one. If you know you'll never get the proposal of marriage you really want, what's keeping you from encouraging another one?

Whether you're husband-hunting, status-hunting, fortune-hunting or job-hunting—*stop witch hunting!* Make up your mind! Then set yourself to the job at hand *singlemindedly* with a will to win!

If you'd like to be a success in business, start working!
If you'd like to be a success as a housewife, start cooking!
If you'd like to be a social success, start smiling!
If you'd like to get married, start looking!

But get your mind, as well as your wardrobe, in order first.

A very successful friend of mine kept her mind on her chosen success goals by keeping a little poem before her on her desk. I don't know who wrote it, but it sums up a true philosophy of achievement.

It may never be mine,
The loaf or the kiss or the kingdom,
Because of beseeching.
But I know that my hand is an arm's length nearer the sky
For reaching.

Whenever any of us tries a little harder to reach a goal—whenever we stretch a little further—we can't help getting a little closer to where we long to be. And even if we never arrive at the rainbow's end, we find ourselves somewhere way beyond our starting point.

Above all, as you take off toward a brighter tomorrow, remember you are an individual. The collection of atoms, molecules and genes that make you are arranged in a distinctive manner that cannot be changed. Your experiment with the paper bag over your head showed you exactly what physical type you are, but you must also recognize your psychical characteristics in order to develop a philosophy of fashion.

It would be jarringly out of character, for instance, for a woman who is introverted, timid and shy to dress herself like a jazzed-up kookie member of the Jet Set. Clothes cannot hide or disguise your real personality. They should be chosen to highlight it, not fight it. What you wear can enhance your personality and romance it, but never change it.

Aside from your physical attributes, your mental make-up and attitude are very much a part of your type and should be considered in developing your wardrobe. An expert make-up man could make Merle Oberon look like an innocent farm girl, but a good casting director wouldn't place her in such a part. Why? Because her public knows her as sexy, sophisticated and glamorous, and an audience would laugh out loud if they saw her being represented as a bucolic milkmaid.

You have an 'image' too, which your public knows. Your public consists of friends, family, co-workers and cohorts. If you attempt to become a brand new and different personality overnight, they will more than likely view you as mad, like Lucia di Lammermoor, rather than transformed, like Cinderella.

There is little question that regardless of what personality type you are the right public relations approach to others is a helpmate on the road to success. While you can't *change* your personality, you can make it more pleasing by trying to please others and saying things people like to hear.

In other words be yourself, but be a better, nicer, more appealing self. And let your clothing reflect that self by making you more attractive to look at.

One more thought before I get back to the workroom. Don't be a slave to your clothes—let your clothes be slaves to you. How?

1. By choosing clothes that *serve you*. They must be right for all the activities in your busy life whether those activities are in the home, the business world, the social swim, outdoors, indoors or taxiing a station wagon full of kids around the town.

2. By selecting clothes that *flatter you* by making you and your figure look prettier, younger, better and more pleasant to look at.

3. By seeking out clothes that are *true to you* in their loyalty to your own type and personality and that build your self-confidence because they make the real *you* feel important.

4. By buying clothes that *protect you* from the dangers of being referred to behind your back as a sad sack, a dumpy frump, a cube or simply as 'my-god-look-at-that-get-up!'

5. By limiting yourself to the clothes that *help you* achieve the success goals you or your family aim for, by pulling with you and for you, not against you, every minute of the day and night.

All right! Get those slaves working! They are the clothes in your closet. If they are just hanging there, send them out to pasture. If they are not devoted to you and to making you more successful, get a new team!

At the beginning of this chapter I reminded you of the time when people wore clothes only for survival. In the space age to come they may again become a means for survival without which we will be unable to breathe, stand the pressure or even walk upon the surface of our homes in space. But right here and now on familiar planet Earth, the clothes you wear are far more than things to keep you alive. They can make you *come alive!* They can be your partners in all the exciting adventures of life. They can and should give you the lift you need for the greatest take-off of all: your launching into the orbit of success.

Edith Head (1897–1981) dressed stars from Grace Kelly and Elizabeth Taylor to Sophia Loren and Audrey Hepburn. Undoubtedly Hollywood's most famous and influential costume designer, Head designed clothes for over a thousand films and won eight Academy Awards. She has a star on the Hollywood Walk of Fame.

Joe Hyams (1923–2008) was an internationally renowned writer and journalist. From 1951 to 1966 he was the syndicated Hollywood columnist for the *New York Herald Tribune*. *How to Dress for Success*, with Edith Head, was the second of 27 bestselling books, including biographies of Humphrey Bogart and James Dean. His cult classic *Zen in the Martial Arts* has sold more than two million copies worldwide.